HONORÉE CORDER
B.HALE

Market
LIKE A
BOSS

FROM BOOK
TO BLOCKBUSTER

MARKET
LIKE
A BOSS

From Book
to Blockbuster

Paperback ISBN: 978-0-9994780-4-2

Digital ISBN: 978-0-9994780-5-9

Interior Design: Christina Gorchos, 3CsBooks.com

Honorée Corder
Ben Hale

GRATITUDE

From Honorée ...

Without the undying support of my husband, I wouldn't be a writer today. Thank you for speaking words of possibility into me every day!

Ben, what a true blessing you are! I cherish our friendship, and our work together is so darn fun it can hardly be called work! Thank you for inspiring me to up my writing game and to write like a boss every day!

To my team: Christina, Dino, and Kevin—ya'll make me look so good! Thank you for your quick and amazing work, I'm blessed to work beside you.

From Ben ...

The list of those who have helped me is as long as my arm, but there are certainly those who've made an enormous difference in my career.

To Honorée, a flawless example of true friendship.

To Kathryn, my editor and ally.

And to my wife, who is perfect.

TABLE OF CONTENTS

A Note from Ben v

A Note from Honorée vii

INTRODUCTION ix

CHAPTER ONE:
What is Book Marketing Anyway? 1

CHAPTER TWO:
Marketing Success Starts with Mindset 5

CHAPTER THREE:
Plan Your Book Marketing 15

CHAPTER FOUR:
Book Marketing 101 23

CHAPTER FIVE:
The Best Book Marketing Strategy (Ever!) 33

CHAPTER SIX:
Evaluating Your Book Marketing 39

CHAPTER SEVEN:
Marketing Like a Boss on Amazon 43

CHAPTER EIGHT:
Marketing Fiction Like a Boss 63

CHAPTER NINE:
Marketing Nonfiction Like a Boss 75

CHAPTER TEN:
Book Marketing Essentials 103

CHAPTER ELEVEN:
Resources: Getting What You Need 123

CHAPTER TWELVE:
You Can Do This! 131

Quick Favor 137

Who Is Honorée 138

Who Is Ben 139

SPECIAL INVITATION

Many like-minded individuals have gathered in an online community to share ideas, render support, and promote accountability. When I first wrote *Prosperity for Writers*, I envisioned helping numerous writers shatter the belief that they must starve to survive. I had no idea what was in store, and the result is an amazing community of 1300+ writers, authors, editors, and more!

I'd like to personally invite you to join the The Prosperous Writer Mastermind at HonoreeCorder.com/Writers and Facebook.com/groups/ProsperityforWriters where you will find motivation, daily support, and help with any writing or self-publishing questions.

You can connect with me personally on Twitter @Honoree, or on Facebook.com/Honoree. Thank you so much for your most precious resource, your time. I look forward to connecting and hearing about your book soon!

A NOTE FROM BEN

M arketing can feel overwhelming for new and experienced authors alike. It was for me. I had a background in small business, and marketing came with the territory, but marketing books is an entirely different beast.

Remember the Courage to Learn law from Write Like a Boss? Well, marketing is another area where you put it to work. Book marketing is an enormous topic with hundreds of methods, each with their own learning curve. When I started, I knew zero—less than zero, actually, because the knowledge I did have didn't apply (but I sure thought it did!). It was a dangerous combination: lack of knowledge and lots of confidence. But what saved me in the long term was my greatest asset: my desire to learn.

When I started, the world of marketing looked like a mountain. I dedicated time each week to study, and I learned everything I could get my hands on. I sought for and studied articles from authors, bloggers, experts, publishers, and everything in between. I did this for the first three years. Most importantly, I never stopped. And that's the key I want you to take from this book: learning how to market books isn't a task to be completed, it's an aspect to your career. Never stop learning.

Market Like a Boss contains the foundation to any author's marketing efforts. Honorée and I have pooled our experience so you don't have to do months of research. It's right here. I hope you're ready to build your marketing foundation and sell tons of books!

A NOTE FROM HONORÉE

W elcome to the third installment in the *Like a Boss* series! Marketing is possibly my favorite topic *of all time* because it's constantly changing and evolving—and I love variety. And, done correctly, marketing is a catalyst to help sell more books. But most importantly to me, by discovering a book, the readers can solve their problem. A super fun side benefit is the opportunity to connect with the readers themselves and hear how your words, in book form, have helped them! That's my favorite part of the whole book business!

In your case, you might have gotten this book because you want to solve the mystery of book marketing. Perhaps you're overwhelmed by the idea of marketing, so please keep this in mind: your book has a long life, and it will need constant marketing *forever*.

So, if you haven't been marketing, or feel like you've done something "wrong," or haven't quite hit the nail on the head the first, second, or tenth time around, all is not lost! The truth is you can keep working with your marketing recipe until you figure out what works the best.

And one more thing: just when you figure it out, it just might change! Google AdWords were all the rage once upon a time, but now we wouldn't even consider using them. Marketing is a marathon, not a sprint. You can (and should) market your book(s) until the end of time, so brew a fresh pot of coffee, grab a snack, and settle in for the long haul. This is gonna be *fun!*

INTRODUCTION

Ben here! We're delighted you are reading *Market Like a Boss!* It's the third in our *Like a Boss* series for authors.

The publishing world has changed, or, more accurately, it has evolved. In the past, writers worked on writing, and publishers worked on publishing. Writers expected the publisher to do most of the marketing. But that time is gone. Regardless of which route you use to publish (traditional, indie, etc.), you will need to know how to market.

Successful authors know how to adjust with the times, and they have learned how to roll with the tide and keep a positive attitude no matter what.

A Change in Perspective, Please

Some might argue that honing your business acumen (I used a big word, do I get extra credit?) means you are sacrificing your art. That knowing how to publish, market, and increase your word count will somehow negate the quality of your work. To those who feel this way, I'd like to pose a question.

Since when does knowledge negate knowledge?

Marketing like a boss begins with a change in your perspective about marketing itself. Marketing does not have to be the tedious facet of business work that you abhor. It can be just as exciting as your work in writing. Let me give you an example.

When my wife and I got married, we had a lot of discussions about what we wanted our relationship to be like. We saw other couples who had their own individual interests, like one husband who went golfing every Saturday morning, or a wife who went crafting with other women. While there is nothing wrong with that type of relationship, we decided we wanted something different. We didn't want parts of our lives to be separate; we wanted to share everything. This discussion led to a decision that has shaped the course of our marriage. We decided that we would **learn to love** what the **other person loved**.

The first few years of our marriage were incredible. I learned to enjoy scrapbooking, romantic comedies, playing the piano, and other things. My wife now enjoys snowboarding, kung fu movies, and video games. (We play co-op, so it's a marriage-building activity.) Together, we've shared every part of what we love. Over time, my interests have become her interests, her interests have become my interests, and we couldn't be happier.

What should you get from this story? That you can *learn to love* something you don't think you would. Remember in *Write Like a Boss* when we talked about the power of a decision? The same principle applies here.

Few authors innately enjoy the marketing of their books, at least not at first. It can feel tedious, overwhelming, distracting, and discouraging. You might work hard and still see low sales, and that can make learning how to market a challenge. Whether you are just starting out or a veteran with multiple books, learning how to market effectively will always be a necessity. Harboring negative feelings toward marketing becomes a poison that will likely stop you from doing it and doing it well. Figuring out how to get excited about marketing and trying new tactics will serve you in a positive way.

Decide early that you will learn to enjoy book marketing, and reaffirm your decision often. Doing so will forever alter your career in a positive way, and it will set the tone of your marketing efforts.

WHAT IS BOOK MARKETING ANYWAY?

Hey, it's Honorée. Before we can tell you what marketing works well and how to do it *like a boss*, it will help you to know what the heck book marketing actually *is*.

So, what the heck is book marketing, anyway?

I'm so glad you asked.

Very simply, marketing is connecting products and services to those who will buy them. Book marketing, then, is getting your books into the hands of readers who will love them. It is identifying the tactics that work the best and strategically executing them for the highest return on your time, money, and effort.

Without proper marketing, you could have the best book in the universe and it would languish in obscurity, making all your efforts futile. And that, my writer friends, would be a travesty. Further, there's no need for it!

Effective book marketing is a magical combination of knowing what your book is about, who is most likely to buy it, who is most like to *read* it (not always the same as the person who buys it—and we'll explain why), where you can and will sell your book, and finally, how you will continuously promote it.

Before you start to feel too overwhelmed, take a deep breath. Come to terms with a few facts:

- Marketing can (and should) be fun

- Marketing can (and should) be inspired

- Marketing can (and should) tap into your deep well of creativity

- Marketing can (and should) always be improved upon

- Marketing can (and should) be adjusted if it's not working (or if you do it "wrong") so you can reach new readers and sell more books

Ben here. I love the list you've given. While marketing can be daunting, it doesn't have to be. We can (and should) think of marketing as an appendage to our writing efforts. When we do, it becomes the new normal. And when marketing is your new normal, so too are sales.

Honorée here. Just as we stressed word count in *Write Like a Boss* and publishing a quality product in *Publish Like a Boss*, we're going to encourage you to develop a marketing habit here.

Marketing must be an everyday, consistent activity. A regular action item on your book business to-do list. If you think I'm crazy, consider this:

McDonald's has been around since 1957. I would guess every single person reading this book has eaten at McDonald's at least once (maybe more than a thousand times). Surely you know where the closest McDonald's is located (even if, like me, you wouldn't eat there today on a bet), maybe even the three closest McDonald's (if you don't, chances are your kids do). And yet, McDonald's is marketing consistently—every second, of every day, twenty-four hours a day, three hundred and sixty-five days a year *all over the world.*

Why?

Because McDonald's wants to sell more hamburgers, cheeseburgers, fries, apple pies, and milkshakes. Every day, twenty-four hours a day, three hundred and sixty-five days a year.

Today is someone's first day at McDonald's—their first visit of perhaps thousands over the course of their lifetimes. When someone says, *Where should we grab lunch?,* McDonald's wants you to suggest their restaurant.

They reach new customers and *stay* at the top of your mind by being consistent with their marketing efforts.

And so should you.

Remember: book marketing is connecting your books with the right readers who will love them. You *can* be great at book marketing, and we're going to show you how.

But first, we're going to give you some insight into *the one thing* that will ensure your book marketing success: your marketing mindset.

MARKETING SUCCESS STARTS WITH MINDSET

(S till) Honorée here. Being adept at marketing is a critical part of your overall success as an author. You've got to play with different options until you get as comfortable with marketing as you are with writing and publishing (even as you sharpen your writing and publishing skills!). The operative word in that last sentence is *play.*

Book marketing can feel unending, overwhelming, and, yes, tedious. Setting the right expectation and settling in for the long term are only two sides of the book marketing success triangle.

In addition to preparing yourself with the right set of expectations and gearing up for the long haul, you would be best served to view marketing as fun!

Yes, Virginia, it can be *fun* to post on social media about your points of view, or characters, or ideas. It is *fun* to attend conferences, connect with and build friendships with other authors, and grow your mailing list (over coffee, karaoke, or other shenanigans). And, it is *fun* to answer fan mail!

Ben here. I totally agree. Marketing is tremendous fun. I once had a reader message me from Iceland. I liked his name so much that I asked if I could use it in a future book. A while later I got another email expressing his shock and gratification. I made a fan for life, and marketed my books, and it was so much fun!

It will help to view learning and trying new marketing ideas as a fun adventure, since marketing requires consistent learning. No, I'm not talking the learning you "had" to do in school to conquer German verb conjugations or figure out complex equations. Because marketing tactics consistently change, you will have the opportunity to experiment with new ideas and learn from others. Just when a tactic seems to become stale, I'll hear about something one of my author buddies is doing and it renews my enthusiasm.

What I'm encouraging you to do is make sure you have a top-shelf attitude, because your attitude determines your level of success. Make sense?

Prepare for Success (and Failure)

Ben talked about perspective and the importance of evaluating a new marketing method. There's one other thing I wanted to discuss before we get into the meat of marketing. And that's hope. You have to keep hope alive, even when it seems like nothing is working.

Ben here. I'm glad you brought up hope, because marketing can be discouraging at times. Even when all signs point towards a successful marketing campaign, it can sometimes fail. But it can also succeed. And, over time, it is not the failures that will define your marketing efforts; it's the successes that will inspire thousands to purchase, read, and tell their friends about your books. When hope drives your work, hope drives your results.

Book marketing tends to have more failures than successes. That is just a fact. Everyone is marketing their books, and there are thousands of new books coming out each month. Some promotions are effective, while others fall flat. That's part of the business, so prepare yourself, recognize when it is happening, and be ready to take it in stride.

Like the inevitable first one-star review (those don't feel particularly great, either), putting time, money, and energy into any piece of marketing that flops is a bummer. Accept now that failure is inevitable, and you'll be ahead of the game. You must market, now and forever, so when something fails, you pick yourself up, dust yourself off, and try something else. Nothing less, nothing more.

Make sense?

The good news—and there is a lot of good news—is that one's marketing efforts tend to:

- Get better with time. The more you do it, the better you'll get. You'll be able to see what works faster and easier the longer you're doing it.

- Increase in their effectiveness the more books you have—if they are under the same author name or brand. This is for an obvious reason: when you market one book, there is only one place for readers to find you. When you market one book that's part of a set of ten, the other books have discoverability as well, and the ability to potentially sell multiple books will increase the impact of each marketing technique. This means that a technique that doesn't work at first might become useful later. Therefore, it's important that you learn about every technique you can, because you never know when it will become essential to your career. As you study this book I urge you to learn, evaluate, and then hope for the best!

LEARNING A MARKETING TECHNIQUE

Ben here: So far, we've touched on how to approach book marketing with a positive attitude, but I wanted to go into more detail on how to learn each new marketing method. With every new marketing technique you discover—whether in this book or somewhere else—I'd recommend you use the following process to evaluate it.

- **Learn.** Always be learning! You can't properly use a new technique unless you truly learn it.

- **Test.** Each new technique deserves a test. I usually only test one technique at a time. Otherwise, it's impossible to know its effectiveness.

- **Evaluate.** You have to measure your successes to determine the effectiveness of every marketing effort. What is measured, improves.

- **Adapt and Repeat.** Many techniques do not work the first time, or they take time to become effective. Don't be afraid to learn, change, and adapt your original marketing effort. Then test repeatedly until you figure out what works.

I use this four-step process every time I start a new marketing endeavor. As you utilize the same steps, you'll find it's easier to identify the marketing techniques that are useful, as well as those that are useless.

Define Success in Advance

Honorée here. Before you turn your laser focus to marketing, you'll stand a better chance of succeeding if you define what you want success to look like *for you.*

- Do you want to be a bestseller or a best *earner*?

- Do you want to add to your email list (by giving away the first book in a series) or sell as many copies as possible?

- If you want to focus on selling, how many do you want to sell—the first day, week, month, year?

When speaking with authors about goal setting, I sometimes hear, *I want to sell* more *books*. But if you sold five more books, would that be what you had in mind? (Probably not.)

As book marketers, we are all hungry for success and yet it can be difficult to attain, especially without well-defined outcomes. This is especially true in today's complex, multi-option book marketing environment where success and failure often live side by side. Many successful authors attribute their success to years of failure (a.k.a. "a time of learning").

The truth is, many of us don't know what success looks like because we haven't set the criteria for realizing or visualizing success. If *we* don't know what success looks like, how can we prove the value of our efforts?

Unless you know what success looks like for you, you cannot strive to reach the point where you can claim success. Failure to demonstrate success will result in dissatisfaction with your marketing efforts, less-than-optimized budgets and poor morale. You might even be tempted to proclaim, *Marketing doesn't work!*

Before you can start planning for success, you must first decide what success looks like.

WHAT DOES BOOK MARKETING SUCCESS LOOK LIKE?

Marketing is the fuel behind any successful book, and great marketing acts like rocket fuel—boosting your book into the stratosphere and catalyzing book sales for a long time to come. Knowing what your book sales goals look like *before* you fuel your marketing strategy is key to actualizing success.

Author's Note: Put the wrong kind of fuel into your marketing strategy, and you run the risk of your book going nowhere fast.

Carefully chosen book marketing tactics, given enough time to work, can equal long-term success.

What follows represents the most common markers of book marketing success:

- **Traffic:** You're looking for quality—the right prospective readers who are ready to buy and read *now*. Quality traffic to your website, online retailers, or other places your books are sold is a vital first step to marketing success. Knowing the size of your potential audience is vital when setting your goals. Knowing the profile of your ideal readers and targeting them with engaging, relevant and timely ads, information, or content will help you achieve your goals. Ultimately, you want to convert quality traffic into readers. The best traffic visits often and engages with you, your books and, if you have them, other content, products and services, etc.

Honorée is right on point here. Traffic can often be measured by engagement. But sometimes it's difficult to measure how many people are responding to your posts. Remember that many few will respond, but many will read. For every individual who responds to your post/tweet/ad, there are dozens, hundreds, and even thousands who read your content.

- **Prospective Readers:** Sometimes, before someone buys your book, they go looking for you and your book (they just don't know it's you they are looking for). Obviously, I'm specifically talking about nonfiction here (but if you are a fiction author, read this anyway as you never know when a gem or idea might strike). Prospective readers are individuals who have a need or desire to read your book and potentially engage with you in a more formal manner (as a client or customer). This is where your persuasive marketing efforts come into play. There are *so many books* available, and you want to cut through the noise and establish that your book is exactly what they need.

Ben here. Fiction works exactly the same way as Honorée has described. A particular reader may go browsing on Amazon because they are in the mood for an epic fantasy containing dragons. They use search terms and look for covers that represent what they are looking for. They don't know it's you they seek until they find your book.

Then they fall in love and become a fan. And that's what we want!

- **Sales/Revenue:** How many books you sell, ultimately, is the end game. If your traffic isn't converting into prospective readers, and these prospects aren't buying your books to generate revenue, your marketing campaigns are failing. Smart book marketers understand how their traffic converts to prospective readers and eventually sales. You will build your marketing knowledge by analyzing historical data and set goals based on trends. You can optimize everything you do by testing and implementing various best practices.

   Ben here. Track how much engagement your post gets and cross-reference it to how many sales are produced for that ad/post/tweet, etc. After doing this several times, you will begin to see a pattern. And once you know the pattern, you can use it to your advantage.

But how do you define your book's marketing success? Take a few minutes and answer these three questions:

- How much traffic do I want and where do I want it to go?

- How many prospective readers do I want to follow my mailing list, my Facebook author page, my Instagram, etc.?

- How many sales do I want for my book(s) [daily, weekly, the first year]?

As big thinkers, we encourage you to dream big and commit to what you truly want *in writing*. Big goals lead to big action. Goals that inspire you will engender you to try new tactics, even as other authors fail and get discouraged.

Michael Anderle set a goal to make $50,000 per year from publishing twenty books so he could live like a king in Mexico. He is a shining example of writing, publishing, and marketing like a boss. Now he has *hundreds* of books and makes many multiples of his original goal. His amazing success all started with a concrete goal, and then he created a book business to be proud of—just as you can!

Ben here. The incredible thing about Michael Anderle's example is that it can be followed by anyone. Set a specific, measurable goal in <u>what you can control</u>. You *can* control how many books you write, how much time you spend on marketing each day, how many posts you will respond to, etc. Setting marketing goals for sales is great, but it's essential that your goals to reach those numbers are things you can absolutely do. The things you can control will influence what you can't.

The great news, which I reiterate, is that your book's life is infinite—even as you determine the effectiveness of one technique, you can always try five new things. Remember to have fun, think big, and stay flexible.

Take some time to define your goals and make sure your mindset is solid. Once your goals are set, we are going to help you put together your book marketing plan, show you the basics of book marketing, and share our most effective marketing strategies with you. Ready?

3

PLAN YOUR BOOK MARKETING

Honorée here. A great attitude goes a long way, but positivity alone is not enough. Marketing like a boss has its basis in a solid plan, which is created before the first post is made, an interview is given, or money is spent.

A Little Planning Goes a Long Way

Unless you're a complete "pantser," you probably spent a good bit of time planning your book before you wrote it. Simultaneously, you found a graphic designer, book formatter, editor, proofreader, and copywriter to help publish your book as professionally as possible (at least, we hope you did).

When Ben and I decided to write the *Like a Boss* series, we mapped out the contents of each book, the timing of each release, pricing for each of the versions (ebook, paperback, and audio), and the subsequent marketing for the individual books and (surprise!) the 3-book boxed set (with bonus content).

Much time, energy, and money go into crafting a book, and it takes a separate set of skills to get a book into the hands of ideal readers.

As you may not yet be a full-time author, have a huge budget, or possess unlimited time, you will have to be as strategic and intentional with your marketing as you are with your writing.

Contrary to popular belief, your marketing plan doesn't need to be overwhelming, stressful, or complex (neither does executing it). Putting together your book marketing plan only requires three things:

1. Thirty minutes or less. Because we're giving you what works, you'll spend less time putting together your plan.

2. Focus and intention. Set aside your thirty minutes and then stay focused until your plan is complete.

3. The ability to decide quickly. Decide like a boss what you want to do to market your business (and be sure to follow the plan through to completion).

To help you quickly and easily create a marketing plan that will work and work well, I'm going to borrow some key questions from my executive coaching practice: What (marketing activities) will you do? When will you do them? How will you know when they're done and if they're working?

The last question is a take on the question of *How will I know?* I don't need to know if your marketing efforts are getting done or if they're effective, but you sure do!

Let's break each question down for maximum effectiveness.

What will you do?

Throughout this book, Ben and I share the very best marketing strategies we know and use—the ones that work. Hint: the best marketing is perennial marketing. Utilizing tried-and-true actions that will work today, tomorrow, next week, and next year (perhaps with slight variations) will be your best bet.

I use a combination of about seven daily activities, which came from hearing Mark Victor Hansen talk about what he and Jack Canfield did to market their *Chicken Soup for the Soul* series.

So, once you've finished reading this book, pick the marketing methods that you will commit to doing and write them down on your marketing plan.

When will you do them?

Once you've identified your marketing activities, pull out your calendar and schedule a time to do them. Just as I write every day from 6-7 a.m. (it's 6:03 a.m. right now), I have a block of time on my calendar every day for marketing activities (today's marketing will take place from 3-4 p.m. and will include updating social media and scheduling podcasts). See the first bonus question below for additional help on this.

How will you know when they are done and if they are working?

Really, these are two separate questions, but they work together (or don't), so you need to consider them together.

To ensure I have an on-going, consistent social media presence, my assistant schedules my social media posts in advance (we use Buffer). I do the "social" (interacting with readers) and she does the "media" (scheduling the content), so I need to carefully review all updates to make sure what's being posted is on brand, appropriate, and follows my social media philosophy. (I'll talk about how I maximize my social media in chapter nine.)

It does no good to just do any old marketing and not measure results. You'll want to notice which of your efforts drive book sales and continue to adjust until you're doing what works—and works consistently.

For example, doing a book tour (going to a dozen or more cities) costs a lot in both time and money. If you only sell a total of two hundred books, but it costs thousands for hotels, airfare or gas, and food, you might be better served doing only local signings and being a guest on podcasts instead.

Ben here. Identifying which conferences are best for you can be a challenge. I'll go into more detail later, but it's important to recognize here that in-person events regularly cost more to attend than you will get back immediately. The value of the connections far outweighs this, but it takes time to fully develop those connections and learn from your new network. Events like Penned Con, Indie Book Fest, and Dragon Con are great for indie authors, but be judicious in which you choose to join. If you're just starting out, pick one to join and get to know the group. You can always expand at a later date.

If you want to become skilled (or more skilled) at reading your data and measuring results, pick up my book with Brian Meeks, *The Prosperous Writer's Guide to Making More Money*, and Brian's book, *Mastering Amazon Ads*. Math and data can be scary and overwhelming but these two books break down these topics into bite-sized chunks.

(They really do. I've read both and highly recommend the content.)

Bonus questions: Two additional considerations go into putting together your marketing plan: *How much time do you have?* And, *How much money do you have to spend?*

How much time do you have?

If you're a spouse or parent (or have any family at all), have friends, work (part-time or full-time) or basically have any responsibility at all, you'll need to pre-determine how much of your "free" (discretionary) time you can devote to marketing.

Lest you just busted out an eye roll and thought, *Yet one more thing I don't have time to do*, consider the fact that you can't underestimate the amount of things you can get done in a focused fifteen minutes. As you'll see in chapter nine, spending five minutes in a Facebook community liking, commenting, and sharing posts; combined with another five minutes adding posts to Buffer; and splitting your final five minutes between publishing a curated list on Twitter and giving some love on Instagram can make a measurable difference.

How much money do you have to spend?

If you choose to engage in Facebook or Amazon Marketing Services ads, or participate in other promotions (such as paying for a BookBub Featured Deal), it is wise to decide *in advance* your advertising budget.

I set aside a percentage (about 2-3%) of my net royalties for advertising. To succeed, traditional businesses reinvest profits so they can continue to grow, and your book business is no different.

In the beginning, you will want to carefully consider where you spend your marketing dollars.

(Although even when you have a million-dollar book business, you will *still* want to carefully consider where you spend your marketing dollars!)

If you are just starting out, earmark even the smallest percentage of your earnings (start with 1% if you have to), and intentionally spend it on some marketing efforts. Businesses tend to grow incrementally, and you can expect your book business to do the same. It will grow faster the more you reinvest in it.

The good news is that most of the marketing we suggest can be done with little or no money. As your business grows, you'll have more to reinvest in not only marketing but also better-quality covers, editing, proofreading, and copywriting.

I look back, as I'm sure Ben does, on my earlier books and cringe. With every book, I strive to get better, and as I earn more, I learn more, invest more in my book business, and, as a result, my book business continues to be more and more successful. Yours will too!

As Honorée said, I actually do look back and cringe. There are many things I wish I would have known that would have had an enormous impact on my sales. In short, I wish there had been a Like a Boss series I could have read to help me understand where to start, and where to grow.

Your Marketing Plan

Because we're awesome, we've created a blank marketing plan for you to print and fill out.

Get your blank plan here:

HonoreeCorder.com/BossMarketingPlan

4

BOOK MARKETING 101

B en here. Now that we've defined the proper approach to book marketing, let's go one level deeper. There are two equally important components to basic book marketing: your platform and your brand.

YOUR PLATFORM

The heart of your marketing efforts will begin with your platform.

An author's platform encompasses every facet of their online presence. It usually includes a website and/ or blog. The blog connects to your online presences, which frequently include Facebook, Twitter, Instagram,

Goodreads, and Author Central. We'll go into each of these shortly, but first let's talk about the purpose of your platform.

The purpose of your platform is to raise your brand identity, give you and your books recognition, and, of course, *sell more books.* Your platform is like a bookshelf; it displays your work. A bigger platform means a bigger bookshelf and more chances readers will find you.

Your Brand

While your platform is the display, your brand is the product. The first question you want to ask is, what is your brand? This question is answered partially by understanding your market. If your market is clever and funny, then your brand will likely reflect that.

If your brand is serious and classic, everything about your brand should reflect that. Decide on your brand, and make sure everything you do is *on brand.*

How do you do that?

You take a step backward and start with more questions. Here is the first question you should consider:

Do you want to brand your **author name**?

Or, do you want to brand your **series**?

Let's discuss examples of each. On the fiction side, we all know Stephen King, Brandon Sanderson, and Jane Austen. These authors are known by their names. Whether by intent or accident, these authors are usually referenced by name and not their books. You'll often hear someone say, "Have you read Jane Austen?" or "Do you like books by Stephen King?" This brand extends far beyond the books and includes their website, their supplementary materials, and their marketing.

Honorée here. For nonfiction, Napoleon Hill, Tony Robbins, and Brené Brown aren't known for their book *titles*. The fact is that they all have multiple books!

Ben here: The second option is to brand your series. Some examples include *Twilight, Game of Thrones*, and *Harry Potter*. You don't often say, "Have you read J.K. Rowling?" You say, "Have you read *Harry Potter*?" In Florida's Universal Studios, you'll find "The Wizarding World of Harry Potter™" not "The Wizarding World of J.K. Rowling."

Honorée here: In nonfiction, you may not know who Tim Ferriss is, but if I mention *The 4-Hour Workweek*, you most likely have heard of that book. Heard of Heidi Murkoff? Probably not, but chances are you have heard of *What to Expect When You're Expecting* (it was even made into a major motion picture!). Who is Margaret Wise Brown? None other than the author of *Goodnight Moon*, a children's book every parent has not only heard of but probably can recite on demand, no matter how little sleep they've gotten! The point is, these authors developed their brands first, names second (or not at all).

Ben here: With the above examples, you'll see the same extension of the brand beyond the book. Everything from the marketing, to television show and movies titles, and everything in between uses the same brand. This is crucial, because it builds brand recognition that will increase your long-term sales.

But Which is Better?

Honorée here: There's no hard-and-fast rule here. We're giving you both options and encourage you to think through your options and choose the one that makes the most sense for you.

Ben here: Honorée is right. It depends on your goals, and this can get complicated. There are so many varied goals and plans that your branding can (and should!) change and evolve. You may want to write under different pen names, series, or genres. But before we get to the complicated things, let's discuss get to the pros and cons.

Branding Your Name

Branding your name (or a pen name) has the benefit of name recognition. This means that anything you write, anything you do, will be tied to your name. If you want to do public speaking, or build a business you are known for, then having your name linked to your books is a great benefit. In addition, if your name is unique or recognizable (like my esteemed colleague!), then the recognition synergizes with your books.

Branding your name has the additional benefit of connecting your brand with other series. This means if you want to write in similar series under the same name, your marketing promotions for anything under the brand will see an increase.

Honorée here: Ben makes a great point—branding my name (especially because it is unique) means I can't ever get away with *anything* so I might as well make the most of it (just kidding). In all seriousness, having a unique name has made it easier for me to brand my name, as well as write on several different subjects.

The benefit of branding my name is that readers have discovered one subject and read each of the books on that subject, leading them to discover my other books. I've had many readers find me through my series for single moms, only to expand their reading into my books on divorce or business development (and vice versa).

You might be convinced you need to brand your name, but wait to make your final judgment until you hear what we have to say about branding a *series*.

Note: you don't have to brand your actual name. You can brand the pen name of your choosing, and even keep your true identity a secret. That will make tracking you down (stalkers are no fun) as hard or easy as you want it to be.

Branding a Series

Ben here: The benefits of branding a series are exactly the opposite of branding a name. If you have a somewhat common name (like Ben), then branding a series might work for you. My fantasy series will ultimately span forty books across several smaller series, so branding the series makes perfect sense.

Branding a series has the advantage of recognition for a world. If you plan on writing a lot of books into a single world, branding the series might make sense. However, this has a caveat. If your series name is overly complicated, that can limit not only the recognition for your readers but also word-of-mouth referrals.

If the title of your series is "Jackson Wilthenium and the Seventy Dragons of Chornasicul," people are probably going to have a difficult time telling their friends about it. (Online dictionaries will also try to tell you those aren't words at all!) The title will also be difficult to put onto banners, covers, social media graphics, etc. It may be perfect for your series, but you may want to consider branding your name in this case.

The other advantage to branding your series is if you want to write *other* content under the *same* name. And this is where it gets complicated, so let's use some examples.

I am writing a series called the *Chronicles of Lumineia,* and the brand is the series. I'm also writing the *Like a Boss* series under the name B. Hale. On top of that, I'm writing a clean romance under the name B. N. Hale. Within a year, I will be writing under three names, but each will have the brand of the series.

Branding any one of my names or pen names would have worked, but in each of these three cases my brand is the series. That said, Honorée has done an excellent job of branding her name, and all of her books gain the benefit because of it. I'll let her tell you about it.

Honorée here. I'm sometimes asked if this is my real, given name. Yup, it's the name on my birth certificate. I hated having a unique name no one could easily (or correctly) pronounce. The boys in middle school sure did have a fun time turning it into nicknames (no, I won't tell you what they were!). Fast-forward to being a grown-up, and I have discovered the benefits of not being one of three Janes or Jennifers in any given group.

It was an even better day when I figured out authors were intentionally choosing unique names to stand out from the crowd. Like I said, if you don't have a unique name, you can choose one (and there are so many cool options!) and brand the heck out of it. The unique name can be the first name, the last name, or both.

Our friend Johnny B. Truant (not his real name) chose a pen name that is fun, playful, and easy to remember (just like him!). You won't mistake him for any other author, and even if you don't know he has a new book out, you'll know it's his instantly.

I think there are two top benefits to branding your name. First, current fans will know in an instant the book they are looking at is yours. Second, you can write in different genres or nonfiction verticals and your readers can follow you as they desire. I was initially surprised when someone would go from reading one of my books in *The Successful Single Mom* series to reading one of my business or even writing books. Now, I make a point to cross-market and always list all of my books in each of my books.

You just never know which of the topics or genres you choose to expand into will be of interest to your readers.

Pro tip: Choose your author name with intention. If I had to do it over again, I probably would keep my identity a secret and carefully choose a fun pen name. I don't regret using my real name, but it is something to consider if you are just getting started.

BRANDING: A CLOSER LOOK

Ben here. Your brand is more than the series or author name. It encompasses color schemes, fonts, style, tone, social media and email platforms, and everything in between. Every post, comment, podcast, interview, conversation (yes, conversation), email, invitation, picture, and book blends together into your author brand. I could talk about myself here, but to be honest, I think Honorée is such a perfect example of branding that I'm going to use her as an example.

Honorée is a genuinely honest person with incredible positivity. Her books convey this—but her brand is more than her books. The way she talks, the way she writes, even the way she looks at you, all speak to her confidence that *you* can succeed. She doesn't just write it, she believes it. She believes in you. She believes in me.

(Honorée here: I do!)

At the same time, Honorée does not believe in excuses. Her brand is that **anyone** can overcome their personal trials and find success and happiness. This is her brand. And if I do say so, it's a darn good one!

Do you see how her brand goes beyond her books? Her covers are upbeat and clear; even the coloring is motivational. All of it is **on brand**. A good brand is natural because it is who you are and what you believe.

But as we've talked about, sometimes an author believes in different things. People are complicated, after all. So, if you want to write in multiple genres, you need to be careful of brand bleeding. I know an author who writes both erotic fiction and children's books, a strange combination to be sure. She has two brands and does her best to keep them separate. Her distinct names are known for their distinct brands, and few know they are the same woman.

We've talked a lot about branding, and I hope you've figured out elements of the brand you want. Keep in mind that a brand will evolve, so you don't need to have everything figured out at the start. You just have to get started. Over time, you will add layers to your brand.

Honorée here: While I appreciate Ben's kind words, I didn't begin with the end or even a vision in mind. I figured it out along the way, using my other business experience and common sense as my guide, along with an insatiable desire to learn. Before you can effectively market, you have to establish your brand. Don't do what I did and try to figure it out along the way, or you'll also experience many mistakes and missteps.

I think because my brand, at its core, is who I am, I didn't make *as many* mistakes (but I certainly made many!). Aligning your brand with your beliefs can be beneficial, and it will also make marketing easy because you will be authentic in everything you do and you won't have to adapt yourself to your brand.

I hope we've started you thinking and that you've made some great marketing decisions so far. Let's get into our favorite (and most effective) marketing strategies— the ones that will work today, tomorrow, and forever. We'll start with the *one* that works like a charm, every single time.

5

THE *BEST* BOOK MARKETING STRATEGY (EVER!)

Without question, we are in complete agreement that the best marketing strategy, bar none, is to *publish another book*.

From experience, we know that having more than one book and consistently publishing new books has been the biggest contributor to our success.

In nonfiction, I advise utilizing the book marketing principle of *the best way to sell a book is to publish another book*, by suggesting the writer's expertise be spread across several books (instead of trying to put the sum of their knowledge in one hefty tome).

How does this work? Tackling a specific sub-topic will allow your reader to solve one challenge, while simultaneously allowing you the opportunity to sell more books to readers who love your style and want your help resolving multiple problems.

As I mentioned, I also have a book series for single moms. In the first book, I give an overview of how a single mom can find her true self again and take charge of her life. I then identified other challenges (such as money, love, cooking, fitness, and getting more education) that single moms face (I knew because I faced them myself) and wrote individual books about them.

If you look at the series, you'll notice that the cover image includes the same lady (a cartoon image of me) in different outfits (a suit, a workout outfit, and a chef's hat and apron, to name three). The stripes on the covers vary, but the look and feel of the books are the same. No matter which book a reader discovers first, they are made aware it is just one book of six in a series, and they'll easily identify the other books they may want to read based upon their needs.

I've sold almost 500,000 total copies of just those six books, and I've more recently compiled them into a boxed set which I sell in only ebook format (the paperback version would be over five hundred pages). The boxed set gave me a seventh book to market, added to the brand, and also provided one more point of entry into the series.

I'm not sharing my numbers to impress you but simply to impress upon you that marketing like a boss means thinking big picture. It is important to consider all angles before deciding your direction and what will work best for you.

Said simply, you *can* make a living with one book, but the chances of that are extremely rare (I know of only one example: *To Kill a Mockingbird*), and I advise against putting all of your chips on one book.

Ben here: The question I get most often is, *What is the best marketing technique?* And it truly is publishing another book. Now, you might have rolled your eyes or frowned at that answer, so bear with me. Let's get to the numbers.

Marketing, at its core, is all about producing sales, right? That means that the best marketing technique would boost your sales, which is exactly what releasing a new book does for your book business. You might initially think launching a new book is not marketing, but let's get into exactly what a book launch does to your brand and ultimately your sales.

Here are just eight impacts of a new book release:

1. Immediately increases total company sales.

2. Immediately increases book sales for similar books.

3. Increases long-term sales for company.

4. Adds another point of contact for readers, otherwise known as an entry point to your brand.

5. Increases sales of future books because there are more entry points for readers to find the new title.

6. The company becomes more resistant to highs and lows of the market.

7. Brings new readers who might not have noticed past covers.

8. Increases brand awareness and therefore followers of the brand. This is measured through social media (Facebook "likes," "loves," and "shares;" Twitter followers, replies, and retweets; as well as blog followers and comments...and we haven't even mentioned Instagram or Snapchat!).

These are just some of the ways a new book release impacts your brand. Other marketing techniques, promotions, or sales cannot match the impact of a book launch.

For this reason, you'll see that most smart authors **pair their marketing efforts with a book launch**. Discounting a book? Good. Discounting a book because a new book is coming out? Even better. As you read the techniques listed in the rest of this book (and beyond!), make sure you look at not just *how* useful they will be, but also *when* they will be most useful.

This is where book marketing really shines—not when it boosts sales, but when it pushes **organic** sales. And this is the true secret to marketing books.

There is no threshold to cross that will enable your sales to be self-sustainable. You can hit #1 in any bookstore, and eventually sales for that book will decline. Again, you need to plan to market your books forever.

All books decline in sales. The decline might be slow or it might be fast; but all book sales will decrease over time. You cannot pay for enough advertising to get, and stay, on top. New books are coming out daily and they will inevitably outsell older content. That's why you need to be smart and intentional with your marketing.

Your goal isn't to rise in sales; it's to create a chance at organic growth. Five promotions scattered throughout the year will be less effective than using them in a group— but not necessarily on the same day. These promotions will support a book release and impact everything else you have already published.

Any book marketing is good.

Smart book marketing is far better.

Understanding how and when to pair marketing with a book launch can have an enormous impact on sales. Now that we've talked about brand and timing, let's talk about maximizing your marketing.

6

EVALUATING YOUR BOOK MARKETING

B en here. Setting your attitude towards marketing aside, let's talk about the actual process of learning. There are thousands of ways to market a book, and we are only going to talk about some of them. The most important thing about book marketing isn't the technique, it's **evaluating the technique** for its potential impact on your sales.

Throughout your career, you will meet authors who use all sorts of marketing methods. The challenge is that marketing is highly specific to the brand and the products. What works for one will not necessarily work for another. In short, there is no "one size fits all" for any writer.

As you read this book, it's essential that you look at each technique as a potential marketing tool that you should learn, master, and then add to your tool belt. Figure out when it will work and when it won't. We have culled the best marketing methods between the two of us, but while they still might not fit into your brand and career, you may be inspired to create something that does!

The ability to evaluate marketing techniques will become even more essential in the future. What will work five years from now hasn't even been invented yet, and that means I'll have to learn it. When that time comes, I will practice exactly what I'm teaching here. I will study, learn, and adapt. Remember the Courage to Adapt law from *Write Like a Boss*? Even we—who have multiple books out and write full-time—evaluate marketing techniques in order to find out the value of their effectiveness.

Every book is different. Every author is different. Every brand is different. But learning how to market is an essential skill every author must master to be successful.

TAKE THE TIME IT TAKES!

Honorée here. As you're learning, testing, and evaluating new marketing techniques and strategies, it is easy to want instant gratification, get distracted, or quit too soon.

In a word: don't.

Many authors expect their marketing to produce results as quickly as instant coffee or microwave coffee, but it rarely works that way. Marketing requires constant oversight and management, and it takes time to make it work.

It takes multiple exposures (impressions) for someone to recognize your name, book cover, or brand. Let me put it this way: there's a reason McDonald's advertises every second of every day, twenty-four hours a day, three hundred and sixty-five days a year, year in and year out. Yes, we (and our kids) know the closest three locations, and they are still putting the word out. Why? Because there is a lot vying for the attention of buyers. Their buyers *and* your buyers.

What I want you to take away from this part of our message is that you need to settle in for the long term. The different between having a book *hobby* and a book *business* is that a business owner is serious and is willing to do what it takes to last over the long term.

Give enough time with each strategy so you know whether it works or doesn't work.

7

MARKETING LIKE A BOSS ON AMAZON

Honorée here. Amazon gets its own chapter because as of this writing (and we believe for a long time coming), it is the 800-pound gorilla of the online retail book world. You will probably sell more on this platform than anywhere else.

Choosing to publish exclusively on Amazon—or not to publish on Amazon at all—is a marketing decision. There are times it is prudent to "go wide," which means you'll publish your books on all online retail platforms. At other times, choosing Amazon exclusivity is your best bet. And sometimes, the best decision is to choose exclusivity for a 90-day period and then go wide (or vice versa).

So, what's the answer? There are multiple things to consider when making this decision, such as your short- and long-term goals, your other books, your platform, your general skill at marketing, your series/stand-alone titles, and others. To accurately help you decide, I'd have to talk to you directly to understand your desired goals and outcomes to accurately advise you. While I do a limited amount of strategic book coaching, this is not a pitch!

Information is power, and without every piece of information available to you, you won't make an informed and smart decision for you and your book. Make sense?

The best we can do here is give you as much information as we can and empower you to make the best decision for you and your book business.

An Amazon Overview

Ben here.

There are several sub-topics related just to Amazon, and I want to arm you with knowledge so you *can* make an informed decision.

Amazon Rankings

An important aspect in book marketing is retailer rankings. Amazon, along with nearly all book retailers, gives books a ranking. The ranking is based on a myriad of factors, some of which include sales, price of book, page reads (in the case of KDP Select), and the number of reviews (plus whether they are "verified" reviews, which indicates the reviewer has purchased the book). Different retailers use different considerations, but regardless of the components, it is important you understand how the ranking works. Only then can you use their system's metrics to your advantage.

First, Amazon rankings are comparative. This means that if you are ranked at 10,000, there are 9,999 books selling better than yours **in that moment**. An hour later, the rank will be adjusted based on the new calculation.

Understanding how to read book rankings is crucial, because sales are not the *only* thing you want. You want the highest ranking possible for your book(s). A higher book ranking increases exposure, which means your book shows up in more places. On Amazon, this usually means your book shows up in the top 100 of its category (or multiple categories), as well as in the "Customers who bought this also bought..." and "Customers who viewed this also viewed..." or "Inspired by your browsing history..." sections.

The best form of exposure comes in the form of bestseller lists, and a new book can be on a lot of lists. You can be in several categories—even ones you didn't select on publication. You can also be on the "Hot New Releases" lists of those same categories. I once had a new release that showed up on thirteen bestseller lists. And those were just the ones I could find.

Getting more sales does not necessarily mean more exposure. If you sell more and everyone else also sells more, you won't go up or down. If you have a great sales day and everyone above you has a *really great* sales day, your ranking might actually go down. I know, it can be confusing.

What's important is that when you do your promotions, you focus on trying to boost your ranking, because doing so will bring in organic sales. Remember, our goal is to increase ranking, which produces the sales you really want.

Learning to read a ranking will also be beneficial because you will be able to measure how other books are doing. Understanding ranking is important in your market research. When you evaluate keywords (also discussed in this chapter), you're going to need to measure how a book is doing. Is the cover good? Maybe. But how is it performing? You won't need to know the sales. You'll know the ranking (when you know how to read a book's ranking, you can ballpark guess the sales as well). So how do you read the sales?

We can't tell you *exactly*.

We'd love to, but Amazon's ranking algorithms change so much that it's difficult to predict an exact number. Although I can't give you exact numbers, I can give you a general idea. When looking at a book, you really want to know, *Is this book selling*, and if so, *How well?* If you want something more specific, just do a basic search for "Amazon ranking calculator," and you'll find plenty of tools that will be accurate in that moment.

Here are numbers that will give you a general idea:

- 100,000+ ranking: Low. Probably selling a book every couple of days.

- 30,000-100,000: Middle/Low ranking. Probably selling a few a day on average.

- 5,000-30,000: Middle ranking. Probably 10-20 sales a day.

- 1,000-5,000: Middle/High ranking. Probably selling 30 books a day or more.

- 100-1,000: High ranking. Likely selling more than 100 books each day on the low end, and hundreds a day on the high end.

- 1-100: Ridiculously High ranking. Possibly selling 1,000 books a day. The top ten might be topping 10,000 sales each day.

Honorée here. Any book in the top 5,000 is selling well. My goal is to keep my books in the top 30,000, because that means I'm selling at least a few a day, which keeps them relevant, places them in the top 100 or even 50 in their best categories, and gives them a better chance of organic discovery.

When you have a book that sells enough, or have enough books that are doing well, you'll also rank in the top 100 in your author category. My business partner, Hal Elrod, usually ranks in more than one category. Currently, he is #16 in the Kindle eBooks: Business & Money category, and #38 in Books: Business & Money.

The Miracle Morning is routinely in the top 1,000 books, and sometimes in the top 100. His increased exposure, based on book sales, keeps the other books in the series (in which I am a co-creator) selling. The sales of all of the books, combined, determines your author ranking.

Ben here. I'm glad you brought up the author ranking. Fewer readers look at an author ranking, but for those who do, it means a great deal. At one point, I saw myself positioned next to some of my favorite authors. Readers can click on the author ranking on a book or author page and find the list. And if you are next to a big name, they may click on you, just because you are ranked next to their favorite author. And that's awesome!

Hopefully at this point you now understand why your goal should be gaining a ranking, rather than sales. You'll be surprised how often reading your ranking will be useful.

As we finish this section, please keep in mind one important thing: there is plenty of room for everyone. Resist the temptation to be upset with an author because their book has a higher ranking. Amazon might rank our books, but that doesn't mean we are better or worse than each other. There are enough individuals tearing down authors for their work. Don't be one of them.

Honorée here. Comparisonitis is the enemy of joy; your joy, to be exact. There will always be another book that ranks higher, other authors who are doing better. Be happy for those authors! They've worked hard to get where they are, and, best case, they are inspiration for what is possible *for you*.

Books in your category that are doing well are evidence that there are readers hungry for what you're writing. No one reads only *one book* again and again—readers want new content, and once they finish a book (much faster than we can produce them, that's for sure!), they go in search of their next, new read.

(Perhaps this would be a good time to stop and get some words down? Smile.)

Keywords are a silent but critical force in a book's success. I'll let Ben share his expertise because you'll love what discovering your ideal keywords can do for your book sales!

Take it away, Ben!

KEYWORDS

Thanks, Honorée! Ben here...

Keywords are a big topic, because they can increase sales automatically when chosen correctly.

The first thing to understand is that a single keyword is usually a keyword string. Said another way, it is a group of words or a phrase someone would use to find a book on a desired topic.

On Amazon, specifically KDP (Kindle Direct Publishing), you can have up to seven keywords. Each one will take time to properly vet to determine if it is working at maximum capacity. Keywords can have a big impact on your sales, and can even alter your chosen categories, so choose them carefully.

Here's an example of one keyword: "assassin action and adventure."

As you can see, this one keyword is four words that make up a phrase, which is exactly what a reader would put in the search bar to find a new book to read.

Choosing the right keywords has the potential to connect a reader to your book. Let's take a deep dive to determine your best keywords.

Grab a fresh cup of whatever you like to drink and settle in. We're going to go through each test to identify the best keywords.

Go to Amazon.com and set the search bar to "Books" or "Kindle Store" (for the digital ebook version), whichever you are testing. Then enter a keyword, and let's see what we find.

STEP ONE: REVIEW THE NUMBER OF RESULTS.

The first test is how many results show up. You'll find this number on the top left in most browsers, just above the categories. A large number indicates your book would likely be lost in the sea of other titles. A number too small indicates there aren't that many readers interested in that category. I like to shoot for a number between 5,000-25,000 (and this is just the first step).

Note: Step one was just a preliminary evaluation of the keyword itself to see how useful it might be.

Step Two: Examine Individual Books.

From here you'll be looking at the individual titles on the keyword results page and, if you'd like, pages two and three. Run each book through the checkpoints below to see how your book might fare with that keyword.

1. **Covers.** Look down a couple of pages and see how your cover will look against the others in your category. Better yet, open an extra window and shrink your cover down so you can see your cover against the other titles. How does your cover stack up? Does it look like it fits into the genre? Will it stand out enough to capture interest? Is it on brand? Does it look as good as the bestsellers in that category?

2. **Price Point.** Once you've compared covers, we move to the next step. Look at the various prices of the books on the first page. Are they free? $2.99? $3.99? If they're all free, and you've set your price at $3.99, that might not be your best idea. You want your book to be a comparable price (or less). Pricing your book well is good because your readers expect to pay around the same price point for similar books, and you want them to be inclined to "buy now" more often than not.

3. **Number of Reviews.** Some reviews are more "clickable" than others to readers. If the top three books have a lot of reviews and the others don't, that indicates the keyword might have room for

new top sellers on the first page. If the top thirty books all have a lot of reviews, it will probably be difficult to crack the first page or two of that keyword.

4. **Ranking.** This one is crucial. Some keywords are very popular, and the top books have a monster ranking. In one of my searches, I found a keyword where the *lowest* ranking was 1,000. The odds of breaking onto the top of that list are miniscule without a book having some serious advantages (such name or brand recognition, and a large marketing budget).

5. **Other Book Keywords.** Keywords are not created equal. A keyword that is also in the title or subtitle carries more weight. If you search for "healthy dog," you'll find the keyword in most of the titles shown. If the same keyword is *not* in your title, it will be hard to place high on the page.

Your goal with a keyword is to try to break onto the first couple of pages. Ten pages into the search won't do much for you, because most people just won't go that far. I once helped a friend evaluate their keywords, and her best keyword put her book on the thirtieth page! Her *best* keyword! Make sure you do your homework, or your keywords will be useless, and you'll be leaving sales and money on the table.

Does that all sound like hard work? It is. Fortunately, there are a few programs that make it easier; a detailed list is contained in the Resources chapter at the end of this book. They can drastically cut the time of researching keywords. Personally, I hate researching keywords, so I use the programs to make it easier.

KDP Select

The Select program is an optional program we discussed a little in *Publish Like a Boss*. You have the option to enroll in KDP Select for a period of ninety days at a time (with the option for automatic re-enrollment).

KDP Select requires Amazon exclusivity, which means you cannot sell your book (in any format) on any other retail online platform (including your own website). However, as they say, "membership has its privileges." There are several promotional benefits to choosing exclusivity as detailed below.

The first benefit is that you are included in the **Kindle Unlimited Library** (KUL). Readers pay a set amount (currently $9.99 per month) to read as many books as they want in Kindle Unlimited (KU), and authors are paid for each page read. (You'll want to check to see what the status of the program is before you enroll. It has already changed a few times since its inception and could change again.)

This last month, I received less than half a penny per page read. That might sound like nothing, but I also had half a million pages read in the month. For those without a calculator handy, I received about $2,000 from Kindle Unlimited alone (across all seventeen titles). That's a lot of income, especially considering that doesn't include direct sales. The greatest advantage to the KU program is that the read-through rate is very high for fiction series. Members of Kindle Unlimited can read my entire series. When they enjoy a book, they devour the rest of the series. And, when you have a lot of books, these page reads really add up!

Kindle Countdown Deals and Free Days

The second benefit to choosing KDP Select is the Kindle Countdown program. Once every ninety days, you can discount your book to as little as ninety-nine cents and have it placed on a special Kindle Countdown Deal page. With a little bit of effort, this promotion can have a significant impact on your sales.

Honorée here. You can also choose up to five days per ninety-day period to discount your book to free. This is the only way within the program to get a free book on Kindle.

You might cringe at the thought of giving away your book for free, but free or discounted books give readers the opportunity to discover your books without a huge commitment—and they could possibly become the super fans we all desire.

The truth is that free books are a perfectly viable strategy for introducing new readers to your brand, your current books, your backlist, and all of the books you'll write in the future.

In business, free gifts are a loss leader. You give something away because the investment is re-paid in the long run. Think of it like a perfect advertisement. Aren't you always saying that if someone would just read your book, they would love it? Well, this is where you can make that happen! We'll touch more on how to use a free promotion later, but for now, understand that it's a key marketing benefit to KDP Select.

Pro tip: Amazon might invite a high-selling title to be part of a Kindle Daily Deal, or possibly a Kindle Monthly Deal. If this happens, it means they want to give your book even more exposure, and both of us would suggest taking the deal (and have done so ourselves)! As we write this, Amazon has discounted Honorée's *You Must Write a Book* from $7.99 to $1.60, which has brought her ranking back into the top 15,000 and her Amazon Author Rank in the top 100 in the Business & Money category.

Kindle Countdown Deals and Free Days have been proven to breathe new life into a book and to an author's overall sales.

THE AMAZON CLIFF

Ben here. Now that we've talked about the basic Amazon program, let's discuss more about the nuts and bolts of America's largest book retailer—and how it matters to you.

New books on Amazon get the benefit of additional promotion—for a limited time. This comes in many forms, such as the Hot New Releases list. But this extra exposure only lasts for thirty days and, to a lesser extent, ninety days. After that, the book is on its own.

Traditional publishers understand this cliff and do a great deal to boost a book on its launch. You should understand it as well and use it to your advantage. A book release is a window of opportunity that allows you to target your marketing efforts. Used effectively, this window can have a significant impact on short- and long-term sales.

Honorée here: We recommend you adopt some of the urgency traditional publishers have when a book is released. When a major publishing house releases a book, it gets twelve weeks to "sink or swim." They promote it in major media (which you'll notice is absent in this book as a viable marketing strategy, and for good reasons), send the author on book tours and out for interviews, run ads on Facebook, and carry out the usual marketing push.

Sometimes their efforts work; most of the time, they do not. The author is expected to do the heavy lifting in regard to marketing their book. If the author has a big platform, the book may sell well enough to hit critical mass. If it doesn't sell well, or even hit a list, the firm cuts their losses and moves on.

Your best takeaway is not what New York publishing does or doesn't do—it is their urgency around doing it. Those twelve weeks—in your case, the first thirty days after release—can get your book enough traction to keep it selling for a long time to come.

In fact, it is up to you to take advantage of that first month and the initial exposure your book will get.

But rather than focus on falling off the cliff, for those first thirty days, put all of your energy into getting as much exposure for your book as possible. With enough sales and reviews, your book's sales can stay strong for quite awhile. Amazon continues to market books past the thirty-day mark if and when sales continue due to organic reach. You, my friend, are the catalyst of the organic reach!

Once your book "falls off the cliff" on day thirty-one, the book will have entered into the next phase of its life—and this phase dies when you do (literally). I know, I know, another reference to the long-term mindset you must have to run a successful book business. Yet I don't think it can be stated often enough. Plan to take the time it takes (and it takes a long time), and you'll be fine as well as successful!

ADVERTISING ON AMAZON: AMAZON MARKETING SERVICES

Ben here. One of the newer but terrific ways to keep books selling is Amazon Marketing Services (AMS). Some of the ads start getting impressions right away (the same day they are approved). Sponsored product ads can sometimes start working almost immediately, providing instant gratification. Other ads, such as the Product Display ads, can take between three and six weeks to start delivering impressions.

In addition, the reporting is delayed, so your ads may be running sooner than they show up, sales may not be attributed for several days or even a week, and therefore the numbers take a while to be truly accurate.

I've seen people comment that they had placed some ads and when they didn't start running and working within a day or two, they terminated the ads (which means they never ran and can never run).

Whether you are running ads on Amazon or Facebook, building your email list, or doing podcast interviews, estimate the amount of time your marketing efforts will need to gain momentum (and then add ten percent for good measure). Be slow to terminate an activity you've pre-determined could work for you.

A Note on Taglines

Taglines are short sentences used in marketing and promotion. Think a single sentence or just a few words. These are highly linked to your brand, so it's essential you consider how a tagline will be perceived. Did you notice the tagline of this book? It's also the subtitle:

From Book to Bestseller

A good tagline can make all the difference to a book. As part of your brand, it can evoke emotion, inspire a click, and lead to a sale. But there's a reason great taglines are rare.

They are hard to write!

Encapsulating your entire book into a single sentence is beyond difficult. But the truth is that it's even harder than you might expect, because there are two types of taglines. Here we're going to break down each type: the long tagline and the short tagline.

The long tagline is usually an entire sentence. It's typically used for Facebook or Amazon ads or other promotional material. Think of it like a miniature book description. It's imperative that every word be selected with care and that it evokes an emotion. Here's an example from one of my books:

> **When you betray the Swordsman,**
> **you invite his blade.**

The long tagline is more for advertising and may be drawn directly from the book description. They work well on promo sheets and other marketing materials.

The short tagline is usually vague and typically incorporates parallel language (remember from *Write Like a Boss*?). Here's an example from one of my own books:

> **Even Fate May be Defied**

Can you see the difference between the long and the short taglines? A short tagline might be placed on the actual cover, or on the back jacket. Its job is to be read at a glance, and it usually pairs with artwork to enhance the imagery.

Understanding when and how to use taglines will work to your advantage. The good news is that you don't have to write them at the beginning; you can write them as you need them. I did a number of advertisements before I used a long tagline, and when I needed one, I went back to my book description to find inspiration. Writing a tagline can be challenging, so here are a few tips to make it easier.

1. Write them in more than one sitting. In my experience, taglines rarely come in a single, blinding moment of inspiration. They get forged into being across several attempts—much like the books they are meant to represent.

2. Start with the idea you want your book to convey. Going for great parallel language from the beginning is like a long jumper trying to leap over a freeway. Try taking a few steps to get across. The idea comes first, then the words, then the parallel language. Don't rush it.

3. Stay open to more than one idea. It is easy to get stuck on or married to one line. Authors who vet their taglines inevitably produce better ones. Tap into collective consciousness by sharing your tagline ideas with your author friends, beta readers, editor, or street team. Their interpretation of your tagline(s) may surprise you, and their additional input might be just what you need to finalize the perfect tagline.

4. Pay attention to tagline's impact across multiple formats. A tagline needs to look good. Why? Because it is usually put front and center, and it needs to stand up to the attention. It also needs

to sound good. Rarely is a tagline spoken aloud, but testing it by doing so will help you avoid miscommunications with readers.

5. Give yourself time (even more than you think you need). Much like a book description, writing a tagline quickly is counter-productive. Rushing to come up with the perfect language is a great way to stress yourself out and not produce a great line. You may even commit the unforgivable error and leave a typo in the tagline (I've seen it done!).

6. Let it marinate. After you've taken a break, come back and review your tagline. Even after you think it's done, come back and look at it a few days later. See if it inspires the same emotion. If not, go back and keep working. Otherwise, good luck!

Once you've got your brand identity in mind, or even well under way, how will you know it's working? Do you know how to effectively analyze your marketing so you'll know what to continue doing, what to do more of, what to do less of, or what to stop altogether?

Hint: We didn't know everything either at the beginning. We started where you are and made adjustments along the way, just as you should.

Honorée here. In the next two chapters, "Market Fiction Like a Boss" and "Market Nonfiction Like a Boss," you'll find strategies that will work for both. We encourage you to read both chapters. Even if you only write fiction and won't ever write nonfiction, read "Market Nonfiction Like a Boss" because you're bound to discover something that will trigger an idea (same goes if you write only nonfiction). In some cases, we cover the same strategy, but in a way that works for what we're writing. Hopefully both chapters get you thinking (and excited to market)!

Ben's going to take it from here, and I'll catch up with you again in chapter nine.

8

MARKETING FICTION LIKE A BOSS

Ben here. If you have a passion for writing fiction, then characters become real. They have an identity, a personality, a voice. That's what makes a good book. Marketing takes your great book and gets it to the readers it deserves.

First, let's get to what makes fiction sell in the first place. A great story compels a reader to finish, but a reader can't love your book if they don't start it. This means that if your book never sells, it's never read. Translation: your **writing does not sell the book**. (The writing sells the second book and builds word of mouth.)

So, what sells the first book?

Let's start with what's most important: the cover. We touched on the importance of a great cover in *Publish Like a Boss*, but the topic deserves a reference here for a simple reason. In the modern world of publishing, covers can be changed. Don't hesitate to re-evaluate a cover on a poorly-performing book. Keep in mind that fiction categories are highly specific, so you'll need to do some research on your category.

Color contrast is your first principle. Visually, sharp color contrast stands out in any setting. You see it in advertising, on television, and at the store. Same thing applies here. Your first step is to find the top five to ten categories that line up with your book, and browse through the books in those categories. What stands out? What catches your eye? Colors that are similar will blend, especially on a small screen, where lots of your readers do their shopping. Think about it: a book cover viewed on an iPhone will be about half an inch in size. The color contrast will make it leap off the screen. Covers without contrast might as well be invisible. Don't let your book be invisible.

Next up is the cover design. The publishing world has changed, with many buyers buying books online, via their mobile devices. This means that covers need to be better than ever. When a reader had time to look at a detailed cover on a nine-inch book, a detailed image worked well. Fantasy books depicted battle scenes with many characters and detailed scenery. Take that same image and shrink it down to half an inch, and the cover blends together. It's no longer art. It's mud. And readers don't buy mud.

Think of *Twilight*. Whether you like the book or don't, the cover is incredibly eye-catching. The coloring, the design—this particular cover is a perfect example of a **simple design** paired with **sharp color contrast**.

Your cover is the foundation of your marketing efforts, and getting it right is absolutely essential in fiction. Ask yourself what emotion you wish to evoke. Excitement? Fear? Desire? Curiosity? By comparing the other covers in your category and following the previously-mentioned principles, you can craft a cover that will evoke emotion and inspire a click.

Marketing a Series

One of the greatest things about fiction is the ability to market a series. Readers who fall in love with the characters and story are likely to read the entire series— regardless of the length or cost. This is a double-edged sword that smart writers learn to utilize to their advantage.

Take, for example, a long series of ten books. The great part with this series is that as readers go through the series, they will inevitably boost sales across all of the books, increasing your ranking, exposure, and organic sales. The downside is that there is only one entry point to the series. In a longer series, it's essential that book one has a powerful cover, strong book description, and smart marketing. It then becomes a funnel that leads readers through the entire series. Remember: *the cover drives the click; the content drives the series.*

The Purchase-Through Rate

Let's say you have a five-book series, and book one averages five sales a day for a month. Book two averages four sales a day in that same timeframe. That means your purchase-through rate is 80%. If you boost sales of book one, you can reasonably expect book two to follow at 80%. (Side note: If your purchase-through is less than 60%, it might indicate a problem with your first book. People are buying it, but they aren't continuing with the series. Above 70% is good. Above 80% is great.)

But what if you have those things?

Awesome! Armed with a solid cover and a strong purchase-through, you are ready to start marketing your fiction. But the foundation is just the beginning. Marketing fiction is about building an avid fan base, and that takes time.

Later in this book, we'll talk about short-, mid-, and long-term marketing, but let's talk now about what it takes to build a readership.

Readers *want* to fall in love with a book, but they *will* follow the author. For example, I really enjoyed the movie *Wonder Woman*, but I will watch pretty much all the DC movies. I am also a Marvel fan, and I watch all their movies.

I love the movies. *But I follow the brand.*

Building a readership in fiction utilizes the same principle. Your job is to convert a casual, first-time reader into a fan. The first step in doing this is obviously the story, which draws the reader in and compels them to continue reading. That's the craft, and our passion as writers. Your marketing efforts enhance your story and augment your business.

We've already talked about branding your business, so let's talk about branding your marketing. As should be obvious, your marketing brand should match your book brand. Everything from taglines to artwork should reflect your content. The following are a few (not all) of the options you can use in marketing fiction.

THE PRICE

Strategically pricing your book is the first technique, and there are several models you can follow. Many authors (including myself) use a discount first model, meaning the first book of the series has a lower price than the subsequent books in the series. You may lose a little revenue on the first book, but if your purchase-through rate is high, you'll more than make up for it in the long run.

A good example is when movie theatres do discount ticket days. Our local theatre does $5 Tuesdays, and it's always packed. But what else is packed? The concession stand. We all know the markup on popcorn is obscene, and so that is where they make their revenue. The discount first model is exactly the same. Whether it's free or just discounted, lowering the price of your first book can be a smart business strategy.

You can discount your first-of-series book short term or long term, and they have different pros and cons. Discounting short term is a short-term boost, but you'll make more per sale between discount periods. However, the ranking of the entire series will also decline between discounts.

A permanent discount for a first-of-series has the benefit of encouraging new readers to try your series. The con is that it doesn't have the urgent feel of a sale, so it will drive less traffic as time goes on.

To decide which is better, consider the **Value of Your Reader**. This is a numerical value you assign to a reader who buys your series. This is going to get a little mathematical here, so bear with me.

First, take the revenue earned from book one. Then multiply the purchase-through percentage with book two and add it to book one's revenue. Continue this with the whole series. If I've lost you, don't worry, here's an example from a trilogy on Amazon.

Book one costs $0.99 with a revenue of $0.35.

Book two costs $3.99 with a revenue of $2.80 and has an 80% drop from book one.

Book three costs $3.99 with a revenue of $2.80 and has a 90% drop from book two.

You'll notice that the purchase-through from books two to three is higher, and that's normally the case. If someone has invested in book two, they likely intend to finish the series. Now, let's get back to the value of a reader. Here's the equation:

$$0.35 + (2.80 \times .8) + (2.80 \times .7) = \$4.55$$

You may be confused why the last part is multiplied by .7 instead of .9. That's because book three is selling 90% of what book two is selling, so you have to drop book two by another 10%, or .1. (If you are a mathematician, you'll see that the equation isn't exact. But to be exact would be overly complicated.)

Now, you might be sitting here saying, "I became a writer so I didn't have to do math!" That's okay. Writing fiction doesn't include very much math—but running a business certainly does, and that's what you're doing here: you are running a book business and understanding a little math will make an *enormous* difference in your long-term marketing.

The approximate value of a reader in the previous scenario is $4.55. This number is incredibly important for your marketing efforts because it tells you what you can afford to spend to gain a reader. Spending $4 to get that reader doesn't leave much revenue, so I generally shoot for half of the value of a reader, so here that would be just over $2.

Now, back to a first-of-series discount model. If the value of your reader is higher, doing a permanently discounted book might be better because in the long run it will pay off bigger. If the value of your reader is lower, doing periodic discounts might be better because you need a higher revenue.

Pro tip: Don't forget that your strategy will need to evolve. When you have one book out, a permanent discount is probably not the best strategy. When you have ten, a permanently-discounted book is much more favorable. Don't forget to evaluate your marketing efforts as you grow.

The Boxed Set

Marketing a boxed set is a perfectly viable marketing method. There are even authors who almost exclusively market their boxed sets. The reason why this works is simple.

Fiction readers are more inclined to start a series that is **already complete**.

How many times have you heard a reader complain that the next book was taking too long? Have *you* ever complained about that? We live in a culture where fans of shows won't start a series until they can binge watch the entire season. There are plenty of readers who are like this with books.

The first thing about marketing a boxed set is a simple question. Does the content support one? Amazon doesn't like content that costs more than $10.00, so if the value of your boxed set is higher than that, a boxed set model may not work for you.

A good boxed set for a trilogy costs a little less than if the individual titles were purchased separately. Take note that because there is no drop from book to book, there is no purchase-through affect, meaning the **value of the reader is higher**. It's also interesting to note that the perceived value is actually higher, meaning that if you run a discount promotion on a boxed set, you'll get far more sales than you typically will on a discounted first-of-series.

A boxed set strategy is especially effective if you have more than one boxed set that are related. Discount one to get huge sales, and then the links will drive a purchase-through into your other series.

Boxed set strategies are also especially effective for short story series. The lowest price you can set on Amazon (barring free) is $0.99. A short story series might have ten separate stories all building into one larger narrative, and the boxed set at $6.99 looks like a steal. However, if a reader reads all ten on their own (with zero decline) the cost to readers is $9.90 and value to you is $3.50. If they buy the boxed set at $6.99, the value is $4.80, nearly 40% more! The perceived value is incredibly high, and the revenue on the boxed set is *also* high. This puts you into a great position, because you make more from the title that costs less to the reader.

ENGAGEMENT

All authors use engagement to a certain degree, but some do it more effectively. Think of engagement like a conversation between a reader and a writer, where the outcome is usually excitement. The excited reader might tell their friends, share your post, or bring your book to their book club. In short, good engagement turns one reader into two, and two into four.

Building an excited fan base takes time but can be the most rewarding in the long run. The requirements are simple: post often, and don't just talk about your books. Post stories about other things that might interest your readers. When they respond, respond back. As time goes on, these casual conversations turn into larger conversations, with dozens of readers responding to your posts or tweets.

Imagine the impact when you have hundreds of readers liking, tweeting, reposting, and talking about your content. The excitement becomes contagious, and it spreads to their friends and their networks, inviting more to come and join. This particular strategy pairs very well with the next one.

Giveaways

Remember, the goal here is to get readers to follow you, not the book. Giving away books can be a great strategy to build engagement (didn't I say it paired well?) and convert casual readers into avid fans. Everyone likes free stuff, and doing giveaways around the time of a launch gets your readers talking.

To be clear, I don't use this strategy, but not because it's not effective. It's because I lack the time. I have a wife and six kids, and I'm currently enrolled in a master's program. Therefore, it's difficult for me to post regularly, as well as to prepare and execute proper giveaways. I use other strategies that work for me.

Pro tip: Don't just give away your books. If you are doing a giveaway, include other things your reader might enjoy, such as extra artwork or swag that connects to your series. I have a series based on a thief and the grand prize was a lock pick set from Amazon. Very cool prize if I do say so myself (insert self-congratulatory back slap here). The key to a good giveaway for a fiction series is to give content that **drives more sales**.

Your goal with a giveaway strategy is to not just get people talking, but to get people buying. Even when you are releasing book seven of a massive epic series, do giveaways for book one, or perhaps a grand prize boxed set. The more first-of-series you have out there, the more people start reading. Even if the winner is an avid fan, they will probably give the new book to a friend, family member, or colleague. Smart giveaways don't just boost a new release, they build a readership.

9

MARKETING NONFICTION LIKE A BOSS

Hey, it's Honorée here. If you have a passion for helping others, you're going to love marketing your book. Why? You can help more people faster than you ever could without a book because your book can be in multiple places at the same time—on every corner of the globe. Pretty cool, right?

Your primary goal, once the book is published, is to get it into the hands of as many readers as possible. Your book will help them gain pleasure or avoid pain (or both), and the sooner they have it, the better!

Before I share the marketing tactics and strategies I've found work the best, I want to spend a moment discussing what helps nonfiction books sell in the first place. While I covered these topics in depth in *Publish Like a Boss,* I believe a brief review can be helpful (especially if you haven't read that book).

YOUR BOOK COVER

We've talked about covers a lot, but I want to reinforce the importance of a great cover. A well-designed cover catches the eye of prospective readers and causes them to give it a second look. Making sure it is on-brand and the best you can get will help your marketing efforts.

Why? For a variety of reasons. For one, because you won't lose out on promotional opportunities (such as BookBub) because your cover looks awful. Savvy readers won't automatically know you're an indie because your cover is lacking. Your sales won't suffer because your cover can't hack it against traditional publishing and indies who have their act together.

Said another way, your awesome cover will grab the attention of prospective readers.

Need I say more?

THE SALES COPY / BOOK DESCRIPTION

If the cover gets the reader's attention, the sales copy converts them to a buyer. In fact, I've heard (more than twice) that a great book description converts better than a great book cover! If your book description is lacking, rework it. You can join groups on Facebook and ask for feedback, hire a talented copywriter, or learn to do it yourself by reading books such as *The Adweek Copywriting Handbook* by Joe Sugarman, or *How to Write a Sizzling Synopsis* by Brian Cohen.

THE TITLE AND SUBTITLE

A great title and subtitle compels a reader to buy the book. To borrow a bit from *Publish Like a Boss:*

The title is the topic *of the book, the subtitle is* the promise. *In other words, your title conveys what the book is about, and the subtitle tells what the reader will get in exchange for reading the book.*

Here are four boxes to check when creating your title and subtitle:

1. Be brief, using as few words as possible. You can eliminate "how to" (that's implied in nonfiction) from your title, along with any unnecessary words.

2. Be specific. Identify your book's topic in simple language, targeting your ideal readers by using words they already know and would use to find your book.

3. Be direct and descriptive. Tell exactly what the book is about (don't make them guess because they won't!).

4. Include any pertinent positioning (if your book is longer, shorter, based in science, has an edge).

A great title can boost your marketing efforts, especially if it is memorable (or easy to remember).

ALL OF THE MARKETING

What helps a nonfiction book sell and sell and sell? Great marketing, of course! Assuming you have maximized a powerful combination of title, subtitle, book cover and your book description, you are poised to sell lots of books.

Every single day, plan to do several marketing activities on behalf of your book(s).

The most effective nonfiction book marketing strategies I've found are to:

- Position yourself as an expert
- Build your bench (the team of people who can help you)
- Use ninety-nine-cent promotions
- Engage with readers and on social media
- Do a giveaway on your website or Goodreads
- Stay in touch with your ART (*Advanced Reader Team*)
- Remember Social + Media = Social Media Magic
- Give away sample chapters
- Build and email your list

- Lead or participate in a multi-author set

- Advertise

POSITION YOURSELF AS AN EXPERT

All experts have one thing in common: *their own book*. Everything I have to say on this topic is in my book, *You Must Write a Book*.

Our focus here is marketing, so I'll assume you already *have* a book you want to market. Positioning yourself as an expert, in addition to having a book, can and should include:

- Being a guest on podcasts.

- Having a solid web presence.

- Building your email list (which I cover in detail later in the chapter).

Podcasts

One of the absolute best ways I've found to market my book is to be a guest on podcasts. You can see a list of some of the podcasts I've been on at HonoreeCorder.com/Media.

On occasion, I ask people how they found me, and fairly often the answer is: *I heard you on a podcast.*

Podcasters always need new guests, especially authors with personality who are fun, informative, and engaging. You share insight about your area of expertise to their audience (and you get to share the interview with your audience as well).

Make a list of podcasts and send them a pitch to be a guest. You'll include information about your book, the topics you can discuss, and why you'd benefit their audience.

Become a podcast guest. No matter the subject matter of your book, you will find podcasts that need expert guests, and you, my friend, are now an author (which makes you an expert). Do a search for podcasts with a business focus, and you'll see what I mean! With dozens of new podcasts born every day, you won't have a shortage of places you can share your knowledge. And, yes, you can even do a search for podcasts in your particular niche and perhaps find dozens who would love to have a new author as a guest.

I love podcasts for several reasons. First, I have knowledge and information that is valuable to the shows' listeners, and my job is to show up and have a conversation with the host. Second, podcasts live forever. You can share a podcast an unlimited number of times and for as long as you like.

Hal Elrod appeared on more than 200 podcasts in the three years after *The Miracle Morning* was released, and the success of the book and his speaking career is remarkable. Before his book, he charged $5,000 for a keynote, and now, 300+ keynotes later, he charges $25,000 or more.

I've done more than 200 interviews (you can find many of them at HonoreeCorder.com/Media), each of which I continue to promote (even long after the podcast episode has been released). While some people want to appear only on big and established podcasts, my rule is that no podcast is too big or too small. You never know when or where your next reader or client is going to come from, and it just might be the brand-new podcast with seven listeners.

A note on new podcasts: If the podcast is successful, fans of the podcast will go back and consume every episode. Don't assume the new podcast with only a few listeners isn't a great place for you to share your expertise. You'll gain interview experience and an interview you can share with others. You win no matter what because you now have an audio you can share to help promote your book.

In addition, some of your fans will want to listen to every interview you do. You can help bring exposure to the podcast you appear on (win-win), and you can find new people who benefit from your knowledge and expertise (also win-win).

It's actually quite easy to get on podcasts. The following are your action steps to appear on as many podcasts as possible:

1. Identify podcasts with the same target audience as your book and expertise. I focus on business and self-publishing podcasts.

2. Send an email introduction, telling the host who you are and what you have to offer their audience.

3. When the host expresses interest, provide them with your bio, headshot, and interview sheet.

4. A few other quick pointers: (1) Be your authentic self on interviews. You have expertise that others want. Share as much as you can as openly as you can. (2) Have a great microphone. I suggest the Logitech ClearChat Comfort/USB Headset H390, which is affordable (less than $30 on Amazon), comfortable, and works very well. (3) Be sure to mention your book (and ask the host to do the same in the introduction and as they close the show). (4) Have a URL you share on every show, such as HonoreeCorder.com/Writers.

Your Web Presence

Your web presence consists of everywhere you can be found on the web. Since I'll cover social media shortly, I'm focusing here mainly on your website.

Even if you're a one-book author *and* you own YourBookTitle.com, I suggest you also have YourName.com or YourAuthorName.com. You can purchase a domain for less than twenty dollars a year and have even a simple template website put up for a few hundred dollars within a couple of weeks.

Think of your website as your little piece of the Universe, somewhere anyone who wants to find you can!

On your website, be sure to include your bio, some photos, book cover(s), blog, media appearances, and links to buy your books (on your website and/or other online retailers).

Build Your Bench

Your bench is a group of people you can count on for support, encouragement, cross-promotion, and friendship. It will consist of other experts and professionals, influencers, and, yes, authors.

A strong bench is going to help you over the long term. Having a team of people who support you, provide a safe place to strategize and bounce ideas, and help you get the word out about your book(s) is invaluable.

One day at a time, one person at a time, make friends! Whom should you be looking to find?

Other Experts and Professionals

Chances are you know others who are experts in your field, or in complimentary fields, you can connect with on multiple levels. As a business coach, I made it a point to get to know other coaches so we could trade best practices, insights, and even referrals.

Influencers

Who do you know with a large platform? Most influencers I know love connecting with other influencers. Masterminding, brainstorming, and idea-sharing are just three reasons.

Other Authors

No one understands the highs and lows of the book business better than another author! Everyone is working hard (and smart!) to write consistently, publish professionally, and market magnificently.

Make it a point to develop mutually-beneficial, win-win relationships with those you can help and vice versa. You'll succeed more easily with a community of people. Now, you might be wondering how to find them and get those relationships rolling? I have an entire book on the subject, *Business Dating*.

But! We won't leave you hanging, so here are a few steps to get you started:

- **Figure out whom you need to know.** Who are the experts and other professionals, influencers, and other authors you'd like to know better? *Make a list.*

- **Find a way to connect with them.** In-person meetings are best, especially whenever you can find a way to break bread (or at least have a cup of joe). Sooner or later, everyone attends a conference! If anyone on your list is "geographically undesirable" (they aren't in your city), request a phone call or Skype conversation. Note: make sure there's something of value in it for the other person. Otherwise, don't be surprised if they can't find a reason to make time to visit with you.

- **Think long term.** Very few people get married on the first date, if you know what I mean. Don't expect the magic to happen right away—it can take time for both people to feel comfortable with each other, and even longer for the right idea to germinate. Just like with your overall marketing, take the time it takes (longer than you think, most likely) for the relationship to mature and the good stuff to happen.

A series of conversations, in-person meetings, handwritten notes, birthday wishes, and other relationship-building activities will do the trick. Before you know it, you'll have a group of people who think you're the cat's meow and who can and will become an integral piece of your overall marketing efforts.

As an aside, industry-specific conferences are an incredible place to connect with others. Ben and I met at a conference one year and then started having conversations that have led to this book series.

Ben here. Sorry to interject, but I really want to point out the impact of this single event. I met Honorée at a conference that cost me upwards of $1,500 to attend. But how much will our collaboration return? With three books already between us, I have no doubt the financial investment will multiply its return many times over. Plus, she's awesome to work with.

The $0.99 Promotion

Honorée here. Regardless of the retail price for your book, discounting it to ninety-nine cents can move hundreds or even thousands of copies of your book.

Yes, I *know* you will only make a measly thirty-five cents per book sold (and acknowledge it doesn't seem like much for your time or knowledge); *however*, you must keep in mind your goal of building your name or brand or series recognition.

The new reader who discovers your fabulous book might look you up, buy your other offerings, or even hire you for direct access to your expertise.

The additional sales will, as we mentioned in chapter seven, raise your book and author rankings. Even as it jumps back to full price, the book's organic discoverability is higher.

Personally Engage

Who was your favorite band, musician, or actor as a kid? For me, it was Shaun Cassidy (yes, I've been around awhile). I got *Teen Beat* magazine (even though I was only seven), carefully tore out all of his photos, and was *thrilled* when a fan letter yielded a glossy black-and-white photo in my SASE (self-addressed stamped envelope) 4-6 weeks later.

Now you, my friend, are your reader's Shaun Cassidy. If someone takes the time to read your book and send you a note, handwritten (or typed) letter or email, then you can only imagine their delight at receiving your response. Even if they "only" follow you on Facebook, taking a moment to acknowledge their kind words (in the form of a comment on one of your posts) makes an impact and leaves an impression.

A good portion of my marketing time is devoted to connecting with my readers, answering their questions, encouraging them, and (hopefully) making their lives easier and better.

Personal engagement on an author's part should start on their first day as an author and end, well, *never*. You're going to get busier, but you're never going to be too busy to meet your readers and fans and thank them for their interest. Right? Right!

Stay tuned for more on this in the section on social media, which is coming right up. But first…

Giveaways

You can easily do a book giveaway on your website or through a site like Goodreads.com.

The goal here is to get your book into the hands of a reader and turn them from prospective reader to reader, from reader to fan, and from fan to super fan. The express elevator from prospective reader to super fan is with a signed and autographed book. A book giveaway can be a great strategy to build engagement. Picky readers love a free book, and when they love yours, they will search for what else you have written or are selling and follow you, your brand, and your career.

I can't use this strategy enough! I *love* giving away books for multiple reasons.

First, I sell other things (products, services, and more), and a free book to a prospective buyer is my first point of entry into their world.

Second, I rarely meet or connect with anyone who has read only one of my books. A free book often leads to the purchase of another book, a coaching session, a keynote presentation, etc.

Finally, a physical book is everlasting and can be treasured, recommended, or passed on. The number one way people hear about a book isn't your desired guest appearance on *The Today Show*. *Au contraire, mon amie!* Books are found primarily through personal recommendation. Readers are friends with other readers. People with challenges they want to solve are members of groups, and when they find a great book that solves their problem, they can become a megaphone of recommendation for your book.

Pro tip: In addition to giving away your books, include something else your reader might enjoy. As a joke, someone created a #cultofHonorée mug, and now I give them away by request. (If you want one, you know what to do!)

You could give away an hour of consulting, admission to a seminar or other event you're holding, or access to a higher-priced offering to everyone who enters the giveaway—or a chance per entry for any of the above.

As Ben discussed in his chapter on marketing fiction, your goal with a giveaway strategy is to not just get people talking, but to get people *buying*. If the recipient is an avid fan, they will probably give the new book to a friend, family member, or colleague with a ringing endorsement. Smart giveaways don't just boost a new release, they also build a readership and increase your super-fan base.

Maximize Your ART (Advanced Reader Team)

Building your Advanced Reader Team (ART) is arguably one of the most important pre-publication actions you can take to successfully launch your book. As we wrote about in *Publish Like a Boss*, forming your ART with the right readers will help you to form a cache of ideal readers that sets the stage for more of the right readers to find you forever.

But what do you do with them after you've sent them the book and they've left their review? Assuming you wrote a book they enjoyed (and with any luck reviewed with an honest—hopefully 5-star—review), you'll want to stay in touch with them!

Your expertise doesn't begin and end with your book (or books). Hopefully you're blogging or at the very least sending out emails to your list on a regular basis.

If you *only* have an ART, I encourage you to transfer them to another list (in your case, a new list) that you stay in touch with on a regular basis. Or, transfer your ART to your main email list.

Add value is the catch phrase I want you to memorize, repeat, and execute. Some authors only send an email out to their list when they have a new book or they are pitching their other wares. *Bad idea.*

I'm a fan of relationships, not transactionships (a new word I've coined to reference people who are just out for what they can get). When someone only reaches out to you because they want something, aren't you annoyed? I sure am! But when I get value bomb after value bomb, in the case of a fellow author, I'm thrilled to help, buy a book, and leave a review. This is called the Law of Reciprocity, and when it is in full force and effect, it can be magical!

There are many ways to add value. Repurpose the content of your book into short and impactful (and conversational) notes to your ART. Expand on an idea you didn't include in the book, share a new idea or distinction, or make a complementary recommendation.

My point is this: you've carefully curated a list (however big or small) of folks who are your ideal readers, and you can and must do everything you can to continue and, if possible, expand those relationships.

YOUR EMAIL LIST

An obvious and easy way to stay in touch with readers is by email. I'm sure we can agree we all receive too many emails, but I am sure we can also agree we cherish and save emails we consider important and/or valuable.

While you will most likely sell the majority of your books on Amazon, sadly you won't ever have access to every single buyer until you help them connect the dots directly to you. In *Publish Like a Boss*, I encouraged you to include an invitation to join your email list in one way or another (by offering sample chapters or a free book or some other sort of giveaway).

The only mechanism of communication you control between you and your readers is your email list. You can build a large social media following (and why not? It's fun!), but those platforms can and will continue to change until the end of time.

Do everything you can to build your email list consistently and continuously. I could write an entire book (*Email List-Building Like a Boss*, anyone?), but suffice it to say there are dozens of great resources available.

Ben here. Honorée is right, and now I totally want to read her email list-building book!

Building a list takes time, so start early. One of my early mistakes was that I didn't think I had the time to set it up, and I didn't create a list until my second year. Start early, build often. And just imagine the power when you have 10,000 people on your email list.

Social + Media = Social Media Magic

Honorée again. Social media can be fun and frustrating, effective and a colossal time-waster (and that's all in the first fifteen minutes).

First, let me recommend an incredible book by my friend Chris Syme, *Sell More Books with Less Social Media* (there's a great and free course that accompanies the book, too). Chris is my go-to source for social media marketing, because, let's face it, I should be sitting here writing, not spending "3 minutes" on Facebook. Right? Right! I digress...

Chris will suggest you use the 80/20 rules in your book marketing efforts. You'll spend eighty percent of your time being social, and twenty percent of your time marketing.

Grab her book and go through her course, and voilà! You'll be selling more books in no time. But I have a couple of important points I want to make about social media, too, and the main one is social media, done most effectively, is split between *social* (the fun, informative, or influencing interaction you have with your connections and followers) and *media* (the selling or "wouldn't you love to buy this?" side).

Social

In a perfect world, we want to do business with our friends—those we know, like, and trust. Your followers won't consider themselves friendly or friends with you without a series of connections that have nothing to do with their American Express card.

Reader and fan engagement must go deeper than a like or share, reply comment, or one-sentence response in an email.

While there are some who think it is ridiculous to share pictures of their cats, guinea pigs, vacations, or desserts, those are just the types of posts that get the most engagement.

Yes, people want to see you in your natural writing habitat (at Starbucks, with your Venti* Pumpkin Spice Latté, your MacBook Pro, and your Bullet Journal), in your Halloween costume, at your child's science fair, or celebrating your birthday. Ask engaging questions, post fun photos and videos, or share interesting information.

In addition to carefully curating your online persona and brand with thoughtfully-selected posts, you should interact with others. Comment on other people's posts, like or love them, and share them. Join groups with like-minded folks and participate.

Your followers feel connected to you when they see you're a real person (just like them), who just happens to write books for a living. This is also known as *the coolest job ever*. And who doesn't want to connect and interact with someone they think has the coolest job ever and therefore is quite possibly the *coolest person ever?*

So, what do lattés and cute cat photos have to do with selling books? Nothing other than everything—they help your readers and fans feel connected to you, like you would be friends with them (even if only in an alternate universe).

And, in this universe, we want to help our friends. Which brings us to the media side…

Media

Said another way, media is another word for marketing (or selling). A smaller percentage of your postings and time on social media can and should be dedicated to sharing your goods! You've published a book, and that's a big deal. Authors are the coolest of the cool kids, remember? Anyway, you want to share images of your book. Take that selfie and post it on Instagram (and use Buffer to make that puppy show up on LinkedIn, Twitter, and Facebook while you're at it)!

Change your profile photos to the cover of your book, even if just for a few days. Post a link a few times a day during the first week of your launch on your different social media profiles.

You have something to sell, and no one is going to fault you when you post it for sale. They will be glad because they are at least friendly with you and they want their friend to do well.

Social Media Magic

The magic happens when your social interaction and your intentional marketing come together. Like I said, your friends and fans see that you have a new book. They will be *grateful* and *excited* you've told them about it. At the very least, they'll congratulate you, at the most they'll share your post with their friends and help you get some traction and some sales.

If you do nothing other than follow the 80/20 rule and increase your engagement, you'll see an increase in your name, face, brand, and book recognition…over the long term.

Pro tip: Schedule blocks of time on your calendar every day or a few days a week to pre-schedule your posts using a service like Buffer. You can schedule posts well in advance across multiple platforms. Then, schedule blocks of time where you just log on "for the fun of it."

WHAT NOT TO DO AND WHAT TO DO INSTEAD

There are *many* social media faux pas, and I'm only going to share a few that will work against you so fast you won't even know what happened.

Spamming and Private Messaging

Two egregious errors I see are social media spamming and using private messages without "permission."

Very briefly, don't just stop in to post a meme or about your new book and then move on. Interaction and engagement are the two keys to success on social media. A fly-by posting is the same as email spam—people don't like it and it won't help you one bit.

A post that feels personal, builds rapport, and (bonus!) makes someone smile is going to contribute to the magic you can create with social media.

I'm always shocked when I get a private message from someone asking me to do them a favor when we don't have a relationship at that level.

Or, when I get a private message that is *actually* a sales pitch.

I used to get all excited! *I have a private message! Let's see what it is!* Only to get a message (a) from someone I haven't heard from in ages who wants a favor, (b) that is sent to a group of people and is of no interest to me whatsoever, or (c) that is a flat-out sales pitch. In a word, *yuck*.

A private message that is just like a text message is great! *I'm thinking of you and hoping you're having a great day!* Or, *I'm doing this cool thing and I'd love you to join me.* Both great.

Stopping by to post something fun or hanging out in your private messages long enough to try to connect with several folks are both great ideas, when done correctly. Make sense? Great! Because I want you to make social media magic for yourself!

SAMPLE CHAPTERS

Back in the eighth grade, Ira Stein (not his real name) got in big trouble because he was giving all the kids in our middle school "candy with a little something extra" (if you know what I mean). He was the first boy I skated with at the local roller rink, and I was devastated when he went to "juvie" (juvenile detention). Ira's marketing tactic was my first exposure to (a) street drugs (which I didn't try, for the record), and (b) marketing with a sample.

I took what is actually a great idea and use it to this day (except my activities are always absolutely legal, in case anyone is wondering). Providing a couple of sample chapters of your book does a few things for your marketing that almost nothing else does as effectively:

- Introduces you to new readers consistently.

- Provides a no-cost way for a potential reader (super fan!) to read your work.

- Adds readers to your list! This one is huge because even if they don't buy the rest of the book, you can reach out and stay in touch (and build a relationship with them).

I prefer to give away two sample chapters, which includes the front matter (Facebook group invitation, Table of Contents, Introduction(s)), the first two chapters, and the back matter (About the Author and complete list of books), along with a link to buy the book in all available formats.

Here's your 3-step formula for creating your sample chapter opt-in:

1. Have your book formatter create it for you, and tell them what of your book you want to include. The cost will be *just a little extra*, and totally worth it! Having your opt-in look just as good as your book will be amazing!

2. Create opt-in and confirmation pages on your website. The formula is simple for the URL: yourwebsite.com/yourbooktitlesample. Example: HonoreeCorder.com/FindingReadersSample (sample chapters of my book with Brian Meeks, *The Prosperous Writer's Guide to Finding Readers*, a.k.a. the perfect complement to this book). The confirmation page directs them to their email for the download information.

3. Create an auto-responder series with your email provider. You'll need three emails: (i) the email with the confirmation link, (ii) the email with the link to download the sample (we use a PDF or BookFunnel link), and (iii) an email they receive a few days later to check in.

Once they've moved through those three emails, they can be automatically added to the email list you use for your regular (blog) broadcasts. Hopefully, they will love what they read, buy your book(s), and then become a regular reader of everything you write!

Ben here. I'd like to cut in and say that developing these strategies takes time. Don't feel like you have to do all of them at once. That would be daunting! As we said at the beginning, evaluate these techniques for their potential effectiveness. Then learn them a piece at a time. Now back to Honorée with her awesome content. (Seriously, I'm learning stuff too!)

Multi-Author Promotions

Multi-author promotions are where authors of similar books in a genre or of a similar topic come together to cross-promote each other's books. I love multi-author promotions for several reasons. I get to promote other authors' books to my readers. I get exposed to new readers. And, I get to populate my Also-Boughts with the right books (we talked about why this is critically important in *Publish Like a Boss*).

You can either create a boxed set, where all of the books become one book and you split the royalties (this requires someone to distribute royalties and involves lots of paperwork), or you can all put your books on sale for one day and cross-promote to your various lists.

The first option requires a lifetime relationship complete with legal contracts and on-going contact. The second is more of a multi-day relationship (with the option to repeat as desired) with no strings attached.

I prefer the second, lower-barrier-to-entry option myself, but do what makes the most sense to you!

Advertising

Currently, there are two main options for advertising: Facebook and Amazon Marketing Services.

I wouldn't consider myself an expert in either, although I do both. *However*, there are two experts I suggest:

Chris Syme and the three books (and free companion courses) in her *SMART Marketing for Authors* series *(SMART Social Media for Authors, Sell More Books with Less Social Media,* and *The Newbie's Guide to Sell More Books with Less Marketing).* For less than $20 including tax, you can learn all about the smartest and best ways to market your book using social media *including* advertising on Facebook.

Second, and equally as important, is my author buddy Brian Meeks' book on Amazon Marketing Services (AMS), *Mastering Amazon Ads.* (We also co-wrote *The Prosperous Writer's Guide to Making More Money,* which will help you to understand the math and data of your author business.) He has a Facebook group and provides customer service to help you really get the hang of Amazon ads. With his expertise, I routinely make a 100% return on my ads.

A Final Note on Nonfiction Marketing

Now that you know the most effective ways to market your nonfiction book, you have the tools at your fingertips to pre-determine how you want to market over the next year or so.

The best marketing is intentional marketing. I work in 100-day increments (see my book *Vision to Reality* for more on this strategy) and plot out my marketing a year at a time with the most activity during those 100-day time periods. During the other sixty-five days of the year, I'm still marketing, just with less intensity (mostly because I'm using those in-between times to rest, relax, and recharge), utilizing tools like Buffer and running ads through AMS to keep the balls in the air.

Please remember a few marketing axioms:

- *Marketing is a forever thing.* You must market your book now and always.

- *Your book is new to the person who has never heard of it, or hasn't read it yet.* There is someone out there (is it you?) who hasn't heard of *Think & Grow Rich* by Napoleon Hill, even though it is a staple in personal and business growth. I've read it probably thirty times (and that's a conservative number) and can recite passages from memory. And, there is someone who will discover it for the first time *today*. The same is true for your book(s), even if you published them long ago.

- *Marketing is meant to be fun.* Heck, the entire book business is lots of fun! But marketing, well, marketing can help you realize your dream of impacting people with your words—and that is just about as much fun as one could hope to have.

After we sent *Write Like a Boss* to our ART (Advanced Reader Team), a couple of the members suggested we create a checklist. An easy reference, if you will, so they wouldn't forget anything and could stay on track. We'll get back around to doing it for that book sooner or later but decided to go ahead and do one for this book right out of the gate. You can find it here: HonoreeCorder.

com/MLABList (and you're in luck, we've created one big list and separated it into three sections: Fiction/ Nonfiction/Both).

10

BOOK MARKETING ESSENTIALS

Ben here. As Honorée mentioned, marketing is a long-term activity. However, there are some things you do at different points in a book's life.

I like to separate and define my book marketing, executing different tactics at different times, as well as into the short-, mid-, and long-term. Some are short-term, meant to boost sales quickly. Others are mid-term and take more time to set up, but produce a more moderate boost as well. Long-term strategies can take years to set up and build upon but can be enormously impactful. I know you've waited the whole book for the best marketing strategies I have to offer, and here they are.

SHORT-TERM MARKETING

The methods in this section are useful in boosting sales in the short term. They are quick to set up and quick to enact, but also short-lived. Knowing when to use these and when to pair them with other promotions can make a big difference on your books.

1. Discount promotion. I've talked about this method in the "Marketing Fiction" section, so we'll just touch on it here. Everyone likes a sale, and discounting your book is no different. Discounting the first of a series can be set up quickly. With just a couple of weeks' time, you can plan and execute a discount. But dropping the price isn't enough. You'll want to promote the discount as much as possible. Otherwise the effort will likely not amount to much.

2. Kindle Countdown Deal. As we've mentioned earlier, doing a Kindle Countdown Deal discounts your book for a limited time. But remember, doing a deal all by itself won't do much. Plan ahead and post wherever you can in order to increase the awareness of the deal. Kindle Deals are great when paired with a book release, and using it on a first-of-series when a second is just out works well.

3. Free Promotion. This looks much like a Kindle Countdown Deal and is available through the Select program. A short-term drop to free can be heavily promoted on sites like Freebooksy.com.

4. Fiverr. This site has tons of services for only $5. It's not just for book marketing, so you'll find

other services there (side note: it is unwise to get a cover designer on Fiverr). Do a quick search for book advertising and you'll find a number of people ready to advertise your books on Twitter or Facebook. Using Fiverr by itself won't do much, but in combination with a free or discount promotion, it can be significant.

5. BookGorilla. This subscriber-based site is much like BookBub (which we'll cover in mid-term strategies). As an author, you submit your book so it can be included in an email to readers interested in your genre. The company isn't enormous, but when paired with a Kindle Countdown Deal, it can create a much larger boost. Remember, you're trying to get organic growth, and combining several short-term techniques can build into a larger impact.

6. Giveaways. Again, we've touched on giveaways as a fiction strategy, but here's a little more detail. Doing a giveaway is a great way to increase engagement or boost a book release. Plan to give a few books/swag that your readers might be interested in. You can have readers enter a giveaway using a site called Rafflecopter.com, and even set the terms of what they have to do to get an entry. They could sign up for your subscriber list, share your post, or like your page. Everyone likes to get a free book, especially a signed copy, so doing a giveaway around a book release can help make your book launch a success.

Mid-Term Marketing

1. AMS ads.

We touched on this earlier, and it stands for Amazon Marketing Services. You access it by going to your KDP dashboard and clicking on Reports, and then Ad Campaigns. Then click on Ad Campaign dashboard.

From here you can create, manipulate, and monitor your Amazon ads. You can create an ad based on keywords, or target specific books. For the keywords, you can put in a list of keywords and track the results of each keyword. For the specific targeting, you can choose specific books you think your book is like, and target them.

Pro Tip #1: Try selecting a variety of keywords. You'd be surprised what will work and what won't. You can turn them off quite easily.

Pro Tip #2: If you choose the product targeting, choose books that are similar in nature to yours. You can look at the top 100 list for ideas.

2. Twitter.

I should preface my comments here by saying I don't use Twitter much. It's just not my style. But like most marketing, I know how it works and how to do it best.

Twitter is a live contact between you and your followers. The secret is to tweet often—and not always to promote your books.

Authors who use Twitter effectively tweet multiple times a day and respond to tweets by others. They forge a relationship with their readers and fans, and when they have a new release, those fans tweet and retweet about it. Be real, and readers will respond to that. Also keep in mind the age demographic of your books. If you write historical fiction, Twitter might not be the best platform. If you write young adult (YA), it might be perfect for you.

Although it takes years to build a dedicated following on social media that's large enough to be effective, I would still put it under the mid-term strategy. This is because it can develop faster than the longer-term techniques. Even with a few thousand followers, you can make a difference in your promotion and brand.

3. Facebook.

This platform is almost universal for authors. You start by creating an author page, which is your main connection for readers to find and connect with you. Before we continue, we should talk about "likes."

At one point, getting "likes" on your Facebook page meant everything. If you had 10,000 followers on Facebook, it meant your posts were seen by 10,000 people. But no more. Now Facebook will show your posts to a portion of your followers, and ask you to "boost the post" (which is a paid option) to reach the rest. This is the same as running an ad, which we'll discuss in the long-term strategy. There are also overseas countries with click farms that will "like" thousands of Facebook pages for a fee. In short, "likes" are an indicator of growth, not the main goal.

The goal on a Facebook page is to build engagement. No matter how Facebook changes, they are still a social platform, and that's what you are going for. Think of it as a digital bookstore, where you go and spend time with people who like to read your books. You're building a community and a following; expect it to take time.

The reason this is on the mid-term list instead of the long-term list is because you need to start it early. It's also very easy to set up and can quickly have an impact. We'll talk about how to advertise your page in a moment. For now, you'll want to get your page set up with quality art. Again, the choice in naming the page goes to your brand. Author name? Or series title?

Another aspect of Facebook marketing is joining social media groups. Readers gather in such groups and like to talk about what they like to read.

One of the best such groups is the Band of Dystopian Authors and Fans. This group is amazing, and the organizers are awesome. I've met them at conferences before and they are genuine, fun, and very smart. The group does promos for new books, and the readers are very engaged. For a group focused on apocalyptic fiction, they are positive and fun.

At one of my favorite author conferences, I went out to dinner with several of the organizers. We went to a Brazilian steakhouse and laughed about eating the roasted chicken hearts. We talked books and favorite series, many of which were written by authors within the group. Just think: every group has organizers like that, and they could be talking about your book around the dinner table.

Pro tip: Avoid groups filled with mostly authors because you'll ultimately be trying to sell to each other, which doesn't usually work. Authors are great to learn from, but not to sell to.

4. Reviews.

Seeking reviews is a time-tested method of boosting book sales. Many authors use launch teams to quickly gain reviews to boost a new book. Others seek reviews by professionals and amateurs alike. The fact is that readers are swayed by a good review. Getting a review by a reputable source can boost your sales and establish your brand.

This mid-level technique takes time to build the connections required to get reviews. Launch teams take time to form. Contacting and getting accepted into book reviewer sites takes time and patience. *Publishers Weekly* is a prime example of one you may not even be able to access without help.

5. Launch Team.

Honorée went into this in great detail, and explained how she uses an ART team to help boost her book from its launch. To be frank, she's done it better than I have, so I have learned a great deal from her on the subject. It's located in the mid-term strategy because it requires time to build an effective ART team, but when it's done, it can have a huge impact on a book launch.

6. Awards.

There are hundreds of book contests worth entering, some with big prizes at the end. Awards can give your brand legitimacy to certain readers, and it always feels good to win.

Connect with other authors of your genre to find out which awards are worth going after. Be prepared to spend a little money, because many of the contests require an entry fee. Try to pick the ones that will have a tangible benefit to sales, and won't just take your money.

The *Amazon Breakthrough Novel Award* was one such contest. They don't have this award program anymore, but it bears mentioning. This program allowed authors to submit a book that ran a gamut of eliminations. The winner got a publishing contract, and the semi-finalists won things as well. Even the quarter-finalists got read and reviewed by *Publishers Weekly*. Contests like this can be worth it. Just be cautious with your time and resources in selecting which to enter.

7. Perma-free.

This refers to a permanently free book. You might balk at giving your book away for free, especially after doing so much work to write it. But if you have a large series, or several books, this method might be extremely effective. Amazon maintains an entirely separate list for free books, and there's a whole world of marketing that's exclusive to free books.

Keep in mind that the purchase-through rate on a free book is much lower than a paid sale, so a couple hundred free downloads isn't likely to get enough movement to make a difference. With that in mind, having a permanently free book is a long-term loss leader, driving a lot of traffic to your books. It has gotten less effective in recent years because there are so many free books, but it's still a viable marketing technique.

Making a book perma-free is difficult, though. You'll have to set the book free elsewhere (like the iBookstore), and then report on Amazon that it's cheaper elsewhere. If enough people do that (and it can take a lot) then Amazon will drop it to free. The book can be switched to the paid category later, but it should be viewed as a longer-term option and not taken lightly.

8. BookBub.

There are a few reader subscriber platforms, but none as large as BookBub. This site sends emails to readers interested in discounted and free books. As an author, you'll submit a request, and they will choose certain books based on a variety of factors. Some of their categories have over a million subscribers. That's right, a million. Getting a BookBub ad is enormous and can send a book into the stratosphere. This one company alone has contributed to authors reaching major bestseller lists like *USA Today* and *New York Times*.

The con to BookBub is in their benefit. They are huge and authors across the globe submit to be included. Some are turned down dozens of times before they get accepted. Some are never accepted.

Pro tip: If you navigate to an author's page on BookBub, you can sign up to get updates specifically when that author is doing a promotion. If you have a lot of followers on BookBub, that might sway those making the decisions to accept your submission. When you do giveaways, link to BookBub so readers can sign up for entries.

9. Conferences.

Going to conferences is not just a way to boost sales, it's a way to grow as a writer and expand your network of colleagues. Keep in mind that on paper you will likely lose money going to a conference, because the costs will likely far outweigh what you are going to make back in book sales. That's normal, so go into the conference with the understanding that the value is not just in the books you sell.

When you are at a conference, look at each reader like they will eventually buy *all* of your books. Let's say you attend a conference that costs you $500 between the hotel and the event, and you sell twenty print books. Your revenue is probably about $60, which on paper seems like a huge loss. But let's get into it.

Let's say ten of those twenty people become fans and read every book you produce in the next decade. If you average two new books a year, that's another twenty books sold per year, which translates into a revenue of another $60 per reader over the decade. Across ten readers, that's $600. But we aren't done.

Let's say those same ten readers tell their friends and family about your books, and perhaps even return to the conference next year with a friend. If each of those ten introduce just *one* new fan to your series, that means you get another $600 from those same individuals. Are you keeping track? We're up to $1,260 right now.

Now, let's say you also branch into audio and five of those now twenty fans love audio. They buy and listen to all of your audio books, generating an additional $200 ($2 revenue per audio book, across twenty books and five buyers).

Now, let's say your ten-fans-that-became-twenty are also leaving reviews. It's difficult to quantify exactly how many potential readers will be swayed by a review, but we all know that book reviews make a difference. Let's say that of the twenty fans, they leave an average of ten reviews each, which averages to two hundred reviews! Of those reviews, one in ten inspires new readers to buy, and of those new twenty readers, ten become fans. The new fans go through the same process again, generating another $700 (Audio is now included).

We're at over $2,000 from selling just twenty books at a conference. Are you starting to see the building momentum? I didn't even mention the opportunities and invites that come up because of a conference, and how many other sales can be generated.

One of my first conferences I attended, I met a group of authors who visited schools. Over the course of the next two years, I visited around eight schools, ultimately selling a couple hundred books—from a conference where I sold just two books.

Attending conferences is a great mid-term strategy, but be mindful of the cost. The example I gave above can pay off the cost, but you still have to front the money. Don't put too much into conferences until you are ready.

10. Book Trailers.

Book trailers are one of the costlier marketing techniques, but they can be effective—especially if part of your platform is YouTube. Video content is also useful on Facebook ads because they get more views than other types of ads.

Book trailers are usually set up through a company, but if you have the equipment and knowledge, you can do it yourself. Typically, this marketing technique involves still pictures and voiceover, but the more expensive trailers include actual video. Be prepared for these to set you back a few thousand dollars, though. I would suggest this technique be considered only when several books are already out.

11. Blog Tours.

A blog tour works just like a book tour—except it happens online. They function by lining up a list of blogs in order. Each posts a giveaway, interview, or other reference to your book.

Book bloggers each have their own following, and doing a blog tour allows you to connect your book with each of their readerships. You can find and approach them yourself, or you can use a company that books them for you. Want to know a company that does it? Post in your Facebook groups for the most relevant information. If you need ideas on which groups to join, check the resource chapter at the back of this book.

Long-Term Marketing

1. Subscriber List.

This is one of the best long-term marketing strategies. It can take years, even a decade, to build. But imagine the power when you have a subscriber list with 10,000 readers. Armed with such a list, new releases can be catapulted onto bestseller lists on the first day.

There are several subscriber services that you can use. Personally, I use MailChimp, but I've heard great things about Drip, which has some of the features MailChimp lacks.

When you have a website, you'll want a page that invites readers to join your subscriber list. As you release new books, you can send the information to your fans, and this group of fans will grow over time. For this reason, it's essential you set up your subscriber list early. Keep in mind that if you have multiple brands, you'll have multiple subscriber lists.

Now, there are two sub-strategies to your subscriber list. Are you going for **Quality** or **Quantity**? Let's talk about both.

Quality subscriber lists have low volume but high engagement. Authors who employ this method will likely not have a massive list (probably less than 2,000). These authors enjoy a high open and click-through rates (CTR), though, because most (if not all) subscribers are actual readers and fans.

Quantity lists have high volume but low engagement. Authors who use this method invite pretty much anyone to join the list, and target those most likely to join—not necessarily those most likely to read. The total number of subscribers on the list matters more than the open and CTR. Quantity subscriber list builders want a high volume of subscribers. It's not uncommon for authors who use this method to have 20,000 or more subscribers, but their open and click-through rates are very low.

Quantity lists use advertising targeted to increase sign-ups—regardless if they are a reader or not. Huge lists still have an open rate, and even if it's just 2% that click on a book release email, the results can be staggering.

Neither is better than the other; what matters is that you pick the one that fits your brand and style. I prefer a Quality list because I don't want to spend a lot of time boosting numbers. I also hate spam emails, so I don't like to send excessive emails. However, I have a friend who uses the Quantity method and has upwards of

30,000 subscribers. New releases sell a couple hundred copies in their first few days. Regardless of which method you take, make sure the emails you send line up with your brand.

Pro Tip #1: Set up automation. When new readers sign up, they should go through a series of emails, each intended to turn the casual reader into a serious fan. Some writers have an automation series that spans a few weeks, while others span a full year.

Pro Tip #2: Give something in return for subscribers signing up for your list, such as a free short story, or perhaps a free book. I like to give a free starter library, which includes two free books and a novella.

2. Facebook Marketing.

This is a difficult one. It can be a money pit and incredibly complex, making it easy to spend a lot of money with little result. However, when done correctly, it can yield new readers and great fans. These two combined equal lots of new revenue. This marketing method is located here because it's only effective when you have several books out. In fact, ten might be a good minimum before you consider Facebook advertising.

Marketing on Facebook can be CPC (Cost per click) or CPM (Cost per impression). CPC means you only pay when someone clicks, and it can really add up. The average spent per click is about $1.65 across all industries. And a click does not guarantee a sale.

CPM is a pay-per-impression model. This means you pay a little every time your ad is shown to a user, even if they don't click. Both methods are viable, but it requires research to determine which will be better for you. Either way, Facebook Ads can be an enormous money pit, so be cautious.

The important thing to recognize with Facebook is that you'll be paying a premium for readers. A good ad will cost between ten to twenty cents per click, and perhaps one in twenty or thirty will purchase your book. That gets pricey. But again, if you look at the purchase-through effect, the reader of a series is worth quite a bit as well.

Here are a few parameters to get you started. First, login to Facebook and click either "Create Ads" or "Manage Ads" (under a drop-down menu in the top right corner) to go to Ads Manager. Within the Ads Manager, you can create an ad that sends people to your website or to your book page on Amazon or other retailer. You might create an ad to build subscribers or perhaps to boost sales.

A mediocre ad will have a CTR (click-through rate) of 5-7%. A great ad will be 8% or better. A good Cost-Per-Click (CPC) should be below twenty cents. Otherwise, the cost of those clicks is too much.

Start an ad with a good image and a snappy tagline. Set it for the lowest cost (probably $5) per day, and let it run for forty-eight hours. Not working? Change the audience. Then try again. Don't get discouraged if they don't work. One time I tried forty-three ads before I got one to work (persistence pays off!). The good news is that they can build over time and have an enormous impact on sales.

3. Blogging.

Plenty of authors blog, but few build it into a business. A friend of mine built a blog discussing Excel spreadsheets. Now, I enjoy spreadsheets, but an entire blog dedicated to the topic seems like a snooze-fest. (No offense, Zenee!) But after two years, she had so much traffic to her website that she was generating a monthly revenue from Google Adsense and eventually sold her blog for $60,000!

The point is, blogs can make money as well as generate traffic to your content. Just like other platforms, you must be smart and relevant. You start small and gradually build traffic as more and more people become interested. You can boost traffic if you learn and understand how Google and Search Engine Optimization (SEO) marketing works, but that too takes time. Regardless, if you love to blog and talk to readers, this long-term strategy might be a perfect fit. Keep in mind that doing this business model requires time, diligence, and posting nearly every day. But it can pay off big time if this strategy works for you.

If you've read all the marketing techniques up to this point, you may be wondering how you can possibly do them all. You can't (at least not all at once!). And that's okay! What's important is that you identify which ones work within your brand. Some will be incredible for you, while others will cost money and deliver zero results.

As we said at the beginning, book marketing is more than just lowering your price and telling your friends; it's about building a brand and promoting that brand to interested customers.

In one of my Master's classes, I met an author who had met a famous author and talked about writing. This famous author said that, *There are times to write and times not to write. When it's time to write, you write like crazy. When it's not, don't force it.* I'm paraphrasing here, but the thought is shared by many of the younger authors I meet. They believe that learning how to write consistently and/or market one's work somehow diminishes the art of writing. This is only partially true.

I've met authors who are obsessed with marketing. One had three books out and was desperate to boost their sales. They thought that if their books sold better, they could write full-time and achieve their dreams.

I've also met authors who believed they couldn't write when they weren't inspired. That they had to wait for inspiration to come. One such author said that they thought it was wrong for publishers to require a writer to produce a book a year.

Both types of writers understand certain truths about writing, but they haven't yet learned a core piece of building a writing career. The book publishing world has changed, and to achieve writing goals, it's essential that writers evolve. We must learn how to write, how to write well, and how to write consistently. We must learn how to run a business, how to market, and even how to do marketing math.

I don't necessarily enjoy certain parts of marketing, but I figure that teachers have parts of their jobs they dislike as well. Doctors might hate paperwork, and pilots might hate the time away from home. Regardless of the profession, an **individual must learn and master all the aspects of that profession**. *That's what makes them a professional.*

If you want to be a professional writer, you will have to learn and master every aspect of the book business. Why? Because that's the job. And that's exactly what it is, too. A job. It can be a job that you love, but it's still a job. Lots of people draw or paint for a hobby, but if you want to build a career as a painter, you need the Courage to Learn.

Honorée here: This is the part where we refer those of you who haven't read *Write Like a Boss* to read it now. We recognize that our agreed-upon position (that you must write consistently and treat your book business like a *business*) isn't always popular. But as authors with more than one million books sold and over fifty books between us, we know what we're talking about. If, a year from now, you're still wondering why you aren't a full-time writer (or at least moving the needle and getting closer), start at the beginning of this series. We don't know everything, yet we know enough to guide you safely and successfully to a goal of full-time author.

Ben here: There are certainly examples of authors who have made it without learning or mastering marketing/business, but in the current publishing world, these are the asterisks, the outliers, the lightning strikes. For whatever reason, they got lucky. I am not that lucky, so if I want a career in writing, I must dive into the profession like my career depends on it. Because it does.

We know you can't leave success to chance, and work is involved. And we wrote this entire series because we want you to join us—because being a full-time writer is awesome!

11

RESOURCES: GETTING WHAT YOU NEED

B en here. Mastering your marketing can be hard (or, at the very least, challenging), and this book is just the beginning. Fortunately, this section is dedicated to resources. No matter where you are in your career or skill in marketing, you'll need to know where to get answers. Here we've compiled a list to help you know here to go.

AUTHOR EARNINGS REPORT

We've talked about Author Earnings Report a little, but this site is a tremendous resource in choosing where to target your content. The industry is constantly changing. Books rise and fall, new trends are born, and sales fluctuate. Watching the market is key to placing your marketing efforts where they will perform their best.

Author Earnings Report will also help you manage your expectations. Your book may be the best thing ever written, but if it's in a genre that doesn't perform, you shouldn't expect too much. Discouragement is just as much a danger in marketing as it is in writing, and constantly expecting more from your results can lead you to a great deal of unnecessary frustration. Manage those expectations so you don't spend too much in an area that won't return that investment.

KEYWORD PROGRAMS

There are a few keyword programs, and they vary in their tools and usefulness. They cost money, but they can cut your research time significantly. Here's a quick look at each and how they can help you choose your keywords.

1. Kindle Samurai. This was the first to come out.

2. KDP Spy. This program has a useful feature because it connects directly into a web browser, making it possible to do quick searches on keywords direct from the internet.

3. KDP Rocket. In my opinion, this is one of the best. Not only does it show numbers, but you can also view covers and other information.

Personally, I use both KDP Rocket and KDP spy. I did try Kindle Samurai first but liked the enhanced features of the other programs. Do your research and pick the one(s) you like the best.

Facebook Groups

Remember when we said earlier that you shouldn't market to Facebook groups full of authors? Well, you can and should connect with authors online (as Honorée discussed in "Chapter Nine: Marketing Nonfiction Like a Boss") and in person so you can build your author network. Chances are, the questions you're pondering have been answered by one of them, and building that network is essential. There are a few groups that bear mentioning.

1. Indie Writers Unite. A large group with a wide array of knowledgeable writers. This particular group bans promotion, so you'll get kicked out if you so much as post a link to your website. Learn and grow. Don't market or sell.

2. Club Indie. Also one that doesn't permit promos. But another great one with a large number of writers. When you have a question, post it here and see what responses you get. Don't forget to be a giver as well, and answer questions you know the answer to.

3. The Prosperous Writer Mastermind. Honorée started this group, and it continues to grow as more and more writers realize they can make a living from their writing. You'll want to be sure and check it out.

4. 20BooksTo50K. We've mentioned Michael Anderle before—he set a goal to write twenty books so he could make $50,000 a year and retire in Mexico. Well, now he makes multiples of that and has an incredible group with more than 14,000 people and there are even 20BooksTo50K conferences!

CONFERENCES

Speaking of conferences...we've talked about the advertising available at conferences, but not about the learning. Conferences are either writer-focused or reader-focused, or a blend between the two. A writer-conference would be one that focuses almost exclusively on the craft or business of writing, with panels, talks, and workshops focused on improving your knowledge. They vary greatly in quality, with some still heavily focused on traditional publishing.

However, a conference with good panels will teach highly-sought-after information. The better conferences bring in veteran authors with a wealth of information, so be ready to take notes. But as I said, conferences are not all created equal. Here's how to tell if it's worth your time and money.

1. Look at the guest authors and do some research. What's their genre? Does it align with yours? Better yet, why are they speaking? Did they just luck into a bestseller status or did they work to get there? Is this an author you think you can be friends with?

Asking these questions will help you identify the conferences that will be of the most benefit to you.

2. Look at the topics. Out of necessity, most conferences focus on entry-level information. If you are there, great; you'll find a great deal to learn. If you are beyond that, you might already know the topics and consider passing it by.

3. What other authors are attending? Asking this question is a follow-up to the topics discussion above. You might not be able to learn from the topics, but you can still learn from the authors. I've been to a number of events where I learned more over dinner than I did in the event room. Remember, you've paid a lot to be there. You're there to work, not just socialize with friends. But that doesn't mean it can't be fun!

4. Where is it? How much will it cost to attend, and what are your travel, food, and lodging costs?

In-person connections cannot be replaced, and even if you only get one idea or meet one person, the time and expense of going to the right conference for you can absolutely be more than worth it.

OTHER BOOKS ON WRITING

Market Like a Boss has a wealth of information, but obviously it doesn't include everything. Honorée has written several great books on writing that will prove useful to you. I've been publishing for five years and still found useful information in her books. There are many books on Amazon targeted to indie writers, and studying them will prove useful in filling in the blanks you may have. Remember, your goal is to master marketing, not just learn it. Here's a link to a few we think are good.

- *Write. Publish. Repeat.* by Sean Platt, Johnny B. Truant (with David Wright)

- *Books for Writers* series by Joanna Penn

- *How to Write a Sizzling Synopsis* by Bryan Cohen

- *Write Faster, Write Smarter* series by Chris Fox

- *2k to 10k* by Rachel Aaron

- *The Writer's Guide to Training Your Dragon* by Scott Baker

- *Mastering Amazon Ads* by Brian Meeks

- *The Miracle Morning for Writers* by Hal Elrod, Steve Scott (and Honorée)

This dozen or so books will give you tons of knowledge and information, in addition to loads of inspiration. Putting great information into your mind consistently will compel you to keep writing and to master your author business.

BLOGS

As you build your network of authors, your Facebook wall will inevitably fill with their posts. Many authors will post links to blog posts and articles pertinent to the writing industry. I recommend, instead of scrolling past them, that you read or at least skim through them. These articles may contain information you know, or they might detail the next new trend. It may reveal an upcoming update to Amazon or Barnes and Noble that could affect your writing or marketing efforts.

Don't forget that the writing world began a revolution less than ten years ago, and the modern world of publishing is still in its infancy. Ongoing research is imperative if you want to keep your career building in the way you want. Your network of authors isn't just there for support; they're also there to keep you informed—and vice versa. More than ever before, writers belong to a community of individuals who need support.

Mentors

Although a mentor acts much like any other member of your network, they do a lot more. In this context, a mentor is an author several years farther down the career road than you. You likely connect as individuals as much as by career goals, and they help you navigate the treacherous waters of publishing. Keep in mind that such a relationship is not forced. You don't go to a conference, meet a bestseller, and then say to yourself, *They're my new mentor!* (Although you can mentally have them as a mentor, read all of their books, and follow or even model their career!)

You may already have a mentor, or you may have a good friend who writes. Regardless, a mentor usually follows a natural progression of an author friend becoming a great friend, then becoming a mentor over time. As much as it may seem one-sided, you give as much as you receive, and help inspire your mentor as much as they inspire you. A mentor isn't just a resource; they are a true friend. Honor that relationship by being respectful of their time, being gracious and grateful, and doing everything you can to help them.

Now you have some great resources to start with, and you'll discover many more! We've got just a few more things to share. When you're ready, turn the page!

12

YOU CAN DO THIS!

Ben here: In *Write Like a Boss*, we talked about the Courage of Writing. We talked about learning, adapting, writing, and, lastly, having the courage to soar. Although they all apply to writing, they *also* apply to marketing your books.

I doubt anyone said to themselves as kids, "I want to be a writer **and** a marketer when I grow up!" I certainly didn't. (I didn't even want to be a writer!) Learning how to market may seem daunting, but it's more than possible.

You may not have set out to be an entrepreneur, but that's exactly what you are. You develop and create content that inspires, informs, and entertains. If you've read our other two *Like a Boss* books, you probably have a business plan, a vision, and goals. You may even have some statements you read or repeat every day in order to become what you want to become. All of these elements are part of running a business. And you have started your business.

Marketing is daunting only because it is the unknown, the unfamiliar, and (sometimes) the unforgiving. Mistakes cost hundreds, even thousands, of dollars. But they also give you something more rewarding: experience.

―――

Two months after I began publishing, I did my first free promotion. The free listing option was relatively new, as was Amazon's KDP Select program. I scheduled three free days and was excited for the downloads to roll in. One of the articles I'd read said that each free book counted as a sale when it comes to ranking, so a few thousand downloads would put my book in a high ranking post-promotion.

In those three days, there were thousands of downloads. (I'd done research and marketed it well.) But when the sale ended, my ranking had plummeted. Through a little more research, I learned that the ranking system had changed only a few months before, and Amazon had created two separate listings: *free* and *paid*. This change meant that, when running a free promotion, a book switched to the free listing during the promotion and returned to paid afterwards. This also meant that the book had *no paid sales for three days*.

Fortunately, word-of-mouth and some quick advertising pushed my ranking back up, and it didn't hurt my sales too much. Three months later, my second book came out, and by then I had learned what to do differently. I did another free promotion, only this time I embedded links promoting the first book into my second book. After the promotion, both books were selling almost twenty-five books a day, a significant increase.

You will make mistakes. Own them. Learn from them. Master the techniques that led to the mistake in the first place. You don't write a book in a day (at least I don't!), and you don't master marketing in a day either. Be patient with yourself, and give yourself room to fail.

When I was a kid, I played chess with my dad and brothers. My dad never let me win, and it took until I was fourteen years old before I beat him. I still remember saying "checkmate" and seeing the look of pride on his expression. Looking back, though I played with my brothers as well, I didn't learn as much. The sting of failure creates the determination to succeed.

I know you can succeed if you want to, because marketing is not nearly the monster it appears to be. It's one topic at a time, one technique at a time. As you add layers of experience, you'll one day look back at what you've done and marvel at what you've accomplished, because you'll see a wonderful foundation to a career.

You can learn and master each of the techniques in this book. Whether you use them or not, you *can* learn them. One of the biggest lies people tell themselves is that they cannot change. You can! I once thought I was lazy, hated writing, and abhorred business and marketing. Now, I'm a disciplined writer with years of marketing under my belt. What's more, I enjoy it!

If you're an introvert, you can learn to be social. If you're scared, you can learn to have courage. If you're a writer, you can learn to be a marketer.

I believe in you because at one time, I *was* you. I didn't know the slightest thing about marketing, yet I wanted a full-time writing career. I wanted it so badly that I dreamed my books were movies. It's a total amateur thing to do, but I did it! I once wrote to a professional author through his website for advice, and you know what he told me? The same things I'm telling you here: to keep writing and keep learning! I remember being disappointed because I thought his advice was useless. Now I've come to know it was the best advice I could ever receive.

Be patient. As we said in *Publish Like a Boss*, book writing is a long endeavor. Be patient with your marketing efforts and let them grow over time. You can't plant seeds and expect trees the next day. I've met several authors who wanted some secret key, an advertising technique that they could dump money into and produce sales. There isn't one. You either work hard or get lucky. As I said, I'm not lucky in that regard, so I'll work as hard as I can. And I'll love every minute of it.

Honorée here. I'm looking at a stack of *Write Like a Boss* books as I write this. I'm about to post on social media that I have some copies to give away, and I'm excited to sign and mail them out.

As soon as my writing hour is over, I have blocked out time to do some social time on social media. Later today, I need to write a blog post, and I'll be a guest co-host on the *Smarty Pants Book Marketing* podcast.

I love marketing, specifically book marketing, and I hope by the time you read these words, you're starting to fall in love with it yourself.

Like anything new and complex, no matter how smart or competent you are in other areas, getting your "sea legs" with your book marketing will take some time.

And! Every single effort you put into learning, testing, and trying new techniques in your marketing will pay off. You'll gain book sales, readers and super fans, and experience. You'll also become confident about what you're doing, a little more as time passes.

You *can* learn every aspect of the book business, including marketing. Before you know it, you'll be marketing like a boss!

QUICK FAVOR

We're wondering, did you enjoy this book?

First of all, thank you for reading our book! May we ask a quick favor?

Will you take a moment to leave an honest review for this book on Amazon? Reviews are the BEST way to help others purchase the book.

You can go to the link below and write your thoughts. We appreciate you!

HonoreeCorder.com/MarketLABreview

WHO IS HONORÉE?

Honorée Corder is the author of dozens of books, including the *Like a Boss* book series, *You Must Write a Book, I Must Write My Book, The Prosperous Writer Book Series, Vision to Reality, Business Dating, The Successful Single Mom* book series, *If Divorce is a Game, These are the Rules*, and *The Divorced Phoenix*.

She is also Hal Elrod's business partner in *The Miracle Morning* book series. Honorée coaches business professionals, writers, and aspiring nonfiction authors who want to publish their books to bestseller status, create a platform, and develop multiple streams of income. She also does all sorts of other magical things, and her badassery is legendary. You can find out more at HonoréeCorder.com.

Honorée Enterprises, Inc.
Honorée@HonoréeCorder.com
http://www.HonoréeCorder.com
Twitter: @Honorée
& @Singlemombooks
Facebook: http://www.facebook.com/Honorée

WHO IS BEN?

Ben Hale is the best-selling author of the Chronicles of Lumineia. Originally from Utah, Ben grew up with a passion for learning. Drawn particularly to reading, he was caught reading by flashlight under the covers at a young age. While still young, he practiced various sports, became an Eagle Scout, and taught himself to play the piano. This thirst for knowledge gained him excellent grades and helped him graduate college with honors, as well as become fluent in three languages after doing volunteer work in Brazil. After school, he started and ran several successful businesses that gave him time to work on his numerous writing projects.

Ben launched his first book in 2012, and six months later he sold his business and began writing full-time. Since then he has published 17 titles across five series within the fantasy world of Lumineia. To date his series has sold 200,000 copies and continues to garner praise from readers. His greatest support comes from his wonderful wife and six beautiful children. Currently he resides in Missouri while working on his Masters in Professional Writing.

To contact Ben, discover more about Lumineia, or find out about upcoming sequels, check out his website at Lumineia.com. You can also follow him on twitter @BenHale8 or Facebook